THE SAMUEL AND ALTHEA STROUM LECTURES
IN JEWISH STUDIES

JEWISH
MYSTICISM

and

JEWISH
ETHICS

Joseph Dan

UNIVERSITY OF WASHINGTON PRESS
Seattle and London

Library of Congress Cataloging in Publication Data
Dan, Joseph, 1935-
  Jewish mysticism and Jewish ethics.
  (The Samuel and Althea Stroum lectures in Jewish studies)
  Includes bibliographical references and index.
  1. Cabala—History. 2. Mysticism—Judaism—History.
3. Ethics, Jewish—History. 4. Hasidism, Medieval—
History. I. Title II. Series
BM526.D36 1985 296.3'85 85-40358
ISBN 0-295-96265-8

THE SAMUEL AND ALTHEA STROUM LECTURES
IN JEWISH STUDIES

Samuel Stroum, businessman, community leader, and philanthropist, by a major gift to the Jewish Federation of Greater Seattle, established the Samuel and Althea Stroum Philanthropic Fund.

In recognition of Mr. and Mrs. Stroum's deep interest in Jewish history and culture, the Board of Directors of the Jewish Federation of Seattle, in cooperation with the Jewish Studies Program of the Henry M. Jackson School of International Studies at the University of Washington, established an annual lectureship at the University of Washington known as the Samuel and Althea Stroum Lectureship in Jewish Studies. This lectureship makes it possible to bring to the area outstanding scholars and interpreters of Jewish thought, thus promoting a deeper understanding of Jewish history, religion, and culture. Such understanding can lead to an enhanced appreciation of the Jewish contributions to the historical and cultural traditions that have shaped the American nation.

The terms of the gift also provide for the publication from time to time of the lectures or other appropriate materials resulting from or related to the lectures.

CONTENTS

PREFACE

THIS BOOK IS based on a series of lectures given at the University of Washington in April 1983, the annual Stroum Lectures of that year. Being public lectures, they are presented here as an historical essay rather than as a full scholarly treatment of the subject. My hope is that non-specialists in Jewish studies will be able to read the book; therefore, some clarifications concerning its purpose and its terminology are in order.

The terms "Jewish mysticism" and "Jewish ethics" are used in this book in the way they are used in the history of Jewish culture: they represent both a body of literature and the content, the specific ideas of Jewish ethical and mystical works. "Jewish ethics" refers mainly to the Hebrew term *sifrut ha-musar*, literally, "ethical literature," the literature dedicated to expounding and popularizing the Jewish ethics that appeared in the Middle Ages. Works of this type were written in Arabic by the Jewish philosophers in the tenth and eleventh centuries, and in the twelfth century they began to be written in Hebrew. A description of this transition is to be found in the first and second chapters that follow.

"Jewish mysticism" in this book refers to the literary works written by the Jewish kabbalists from the end of the twelfth century onward, with the exception of chapter 3, which deals with another Jewish mystical movement, the pietists in the Rhineland in the twelfth and thirteenth centuries who were known as the Ashkenazi Hasidim. The Kabbalah, however, was the main form of Jewish mysticism throughout the Middle Ages and into modern times, and the symbolism it used became the standard language of Jewish mysticism. In chapter 2 I describe the process that led the early kabbalists in the thirteenth century to begin to write works dedicated to ethics, and in chapter 4 I discuss the process that led to the appearance of mystical Jewish ethics, the fusion between mystical literature and ethical literature in Safed in the sixteenth century. Chapter 5 is dedicated to a brief survey of some more modern developments: the Sabbatian mystical heresy in the seventeenth century, and the new Hasidic movement of the eighteenth century.

As far as the content is concerned, Hebrew ethical literature is dedicated to explaining the philosophical, or mystical, reasons why a man should follow the ethical demands of Jewish law and tradition as formulated in the Bible, in the Talmud, and in the Jewish legal tradition, the halakhah. The main purpose of the writers of this literature is to instruct a person not what to do, but what to feel and what to believe in while performing the ethical demands. This, therefore, is an ideological literature, which is based on a detailed world view; it can be rationalistic, or pietistic, or mystical, and it will be used to provide an ideological and religious basis for the actual ethical actions.

Jewish mysticism, like any other mysticism, is based on the deep religious belief that divine truth can be neither found nor expressed in worldly terms. Divine truth lies in a mystical realm, completely hidden from human senses and rationalistic analysis. It can be reached only by the mystic, in a way that cannot be described in sensual or rational terms. God, however, gave man some hints of this esoteric realm in the Scriptures, which, even though written in words, refer to a dimension that is beyond human language. The only bridge between language and the mystical realm of divine truth is the symbol, a term of language which expounds not what is known, but what is unknown. A symbol, in a mystical context, is the maximum possible approach that language can achieve toward a truth which in itself can never be reached, which lies eternally beyond human understanding and expression. The symbol is sometimes described as the tip of an iceberg, which can be viewed, whereas the iceberg as a whole is completely hidden. The visible part belongs to the iceberg, it is part of it, but it should not be mistaken for the iceberg itself. The kabbalist perceives the whole body of the Scriptures, and every word in it, as such a symbol, which should not be taken literally but as a remote hint at great secrets never to be known or expressed by man. On this basis the Kabbalah, which began its development at the end of the twelfth century in Provence, and continued in the thirteenth century in a series of centers in northern Spain, created a system of symbols that profoundly influenced Jewish culture as a whole, especially after the greatest work of Jewish mysticism, the book *Zohar* ("The Book of Brightness"), was written in Spain by Rabbi Moses de Leon at the end of the thirteenth century.

There is no inherent connection between mysticism and ethics; it can even be said that there is a barrier between them. Mysticism appeals to the elect, to the few, and is usually esoteric; ethics are directed toward all the people, instructing and teaching everyday norms. The story told in the following chapters describes how these two separated realms first became connected and then, in the sixteenth century, were united, to become one of the most important spiritual forces that shaped Jewish culture in the modern period.

My study of both Jewish ethics and Jewish mysticism began nearly thirty years ago, under the tutelage of Professor Isaiah Tishby. Many of the basic ideas used in this book are based on his lectures and the frequent discussions we had on these subjects. My thanks are offered to Samuel and Althea Stroum and the Stroum Foundation for their interest in the subject, in the lectures, and in this book. I would also like to thank my friends in the University of Washington Jewish Studies Program, especially Professor Stephen Benin, for their assistance, and the University of Washington Press and its editor-in-chief, Naomi Pascal, without whose continuous efforts this book could not have been written and published.

Seattle, May 1985

JEWISH
MYSTICISM
and
JEWISH
ETHICS

1

THE ENIGMA OF
HEBREW ETHICAL LITERATURE

I

THE MAIN SUBJECT of this book is the story of an ideological miracle: it is the tale of seven hundred years of diverse Jewish theological creativity, including many extreme, radical and even seemingly heretical schools of thought, which were integrated into a constructive, traditional Jewish ethics within the framework of Hebrew ethical literature. It is an almost unbelievable phenomenon, that the most far-reaching and revolutionary theological and mystical ideas produced by Jewish thinkers in the Middle Ages and early modern times were collected and re-presented as ethical ideas, and continued their existence within Jewish ethics side by side with the most orthodox, traditional and conformist attitudes. The ability of Jewish ethics to absorb and sustain conflicting ideas, which originated in schools that fought each other fiercely, is most remarkable and presents a fascinating chapter in the history of Jewish ideas.[1]

The following chapters will survey some examples that convey the central characteristic of Hebrew ethical literature: the ability to absorb ideas and presentations from the most heretical, revolutionary, and extreme fringes of Jewish thought and integrate them into the mainstream of Jewish thought and religious practice.

The ethical works written by the followers of the false messiah, Sabbatai Zevi, in the late seventeenth century and during the eighteenth century, constitute the most extreme example of this process, in which Jewish mystical-heretical writers produced ethical literature which was accepted and followed by the orthodox majority of the Jewish people.[2] The situation in the Middle Ages was no different. A clear example is the rationalistic system of the early Jewish philosophers in the tenth to twelfth centuries, when Jewish theology was integrated with Greek philosophy received through Arabic philosophical works, and became a part of Hebrew ethical literature centuries after the schools of the philosophers were rejected by Jewish theologians and replaced by less rationalistic and more mystical attitudes. The revolutionary, mythological ideas of the medieval kabbalists were transformed into orthodox systems of ethics. The revolutionary new ethics of Rabbi Judah the Pious, the great leader of the Ashkenazi Hasidic movement in the twelfth to thirteenth centuries, became an integral part of the history of Jewish ethics, read and followed by his opponents as well as by his supporters. The radical new mysticism of Isaac Luria in Safed in the sixteenth century became the source of a vast new ethical system which dominated early modern Jewish theories of ethics, and the various sects of the modern Hasidic movement were integrated into one seemingly united ethical system.

The purpose of this brief study is to analyze a few examples of this process, with emphasis on the mystical ones, and thus investigate the basic characteristics of Hebrew ethical literature and moralistic norms, in order to achieve better understanding of the history and development of Jewish ethical and mystical ideas.

II

One of the sources of the extraordinary power of Hebrew ethical literature is its continuity. From biblical times up to and including the twentieth century, creativity in this field has never ceased. Dramatic changes occurred both in content and in literary styles and genres, but the basic attitudes of this literature remained. There is only one other field of Jewish religious creativity which can be compared to that of ethics—the literature of the halakhah, Jewish religious law. All other ways in which Jews expressed their religious ideas and feelings are temporary, restricted by chronology and geography. Only halakhah and ethics are universal and constant.[3]

Biblical literature includes works that can be characterized as works of ethics, that is, dealing with the practical consequences of religious adherence in the realm of daily behavior both between man and God and between man and men, ritualistic as well as social ethics. The Book of Proverbs, for instance, can be described as a work of ethics, and it influenced the post-biblical period in works ranging from Ecclesiasticus (Ben Sira) to one of the Dead Sea Scrolls, the Manual of the Discipline of the Sect (*Serakh ha-Yahad*).

Talmudic and midrashic literature, which includes almost all Jewish literary output from the first century C.E. to the seventh century or even later, is dedicated mainly to these two subjects: halakhah and ethics, when the ethical teachings are central to the "aggadah" or "midrash" part of this vast literature. Though many other subjects are included, moral ideas and standards are the main theme in the non-halakhic parts of this literature.

The distinction among talmudic law, halakhah, and talmudic-midrashic ethics is a very difficult one. On the one hand, the halakhah includes ethical considerations in the center of its deliberations, and when the law is decided it reflects the ethical attitudes of its formulators. Biblical verses and ancient traditions are compared in the pages of the Talmud, and a solution to the legal problem under consideration is sought when the goal usually is to reconcile the result of strict exegesis of the sources with the demands of social and religious ethics. Thus it can be claimed that Jewish law and Jewish ethics are indeed one and the same. In fact, if we follow general definitions of the meaning of ethics, there is no doubt that the enormous edifice of Jewish law, constructed by scores of generations of scholars interpreting and reinterpreting their sources and creating a vast system of detailed instructions concerning every facet of a human's behavior toward his God and toward his fellow men, on the principles of justice, fairness, and respect for the rights of the individual, as well as in conformity with God's demands from man, is a clear example of a comprehensive system of ethical behavior.

Even so, the ethics in the talmudic-midrashic aggadah is a different discipline from the halakhah, though both of them are expressions of the great achievement of the ancient rabbis in directing Jewish life and behavior by ethical principles. The halakhah, being a legal system, strives to present the required minimum necessary for the accomplishment of a certain commandment, so that the individual performing it will be certain that he had conformed to the religious and social standards that the Jewish faith imposes on him. The Talmud, therefore, points out what is the minimum height of a *sukkah* (tabernacle), or the minimum amount to be donated to charity. The aggadah, on the other hand, is concerned with the maximum religious and ethical achievement that an individual can attain: it points out tasks and needs without limit, which enable the believer, if he so chooses, to advance toward perfection, both in the human and in the devotional-religious fields. The usual reference to ethics in ancient and medieval literature is *"lifnim mi-shurat ha-din,"* "beyond what the law requires." The halakhah defines the obligatory minimum; ethics, and the aggadah, describe the unending road toward perfection.

Another element that creates a meaningful distinction between halakhah and aggadah is the source of authority. The halakhist, though motivated by ethical, religious, and contemporary social needs, must base his legal conclusion on the strict exegesis of the Torah in ways clearly defined by Jewish tradition. He does not have to explain the reasons behind the decision; but he must show how his conclusion is the direct result of the correct exegesis of the ancient, holy texts. The homilist of the aggadah also relies on the biblical texts and bases his conclusion on them; but to that he adds an explanation of the ideological, ethical, and religious reasons for his demands. The law does not need a justification beyond itself; if it is a conclusion legitimately springing from the Torah dictated to

Moses by God, its motivations may be of interest, but they do not affect its authority as law. Ethical instructions of the aggadah may be illustrated by references to biblical verses, but their power to transform the lives of people rests on their ability to convince the listeners and the readers that this indeed is the just and fair way to behave, or that this is really the correct way to approach God. Hence, one of the most important characteristics of Jewish ethics from talmudic times to the modern age is the emphasis on explanation and inducement, rather than the simple statement of the actions that should be performed.

These are two basic differences between Jewish law and Jewish ethics; but an important characteristic unites them: the complete absence of any differentiation between social demands and ritualistic-religious ones. In Judaism, man's behavior in all its aspects is regulated by divine revelation. The message God sent to his people by means of the Torah and the prophets does not distinguish between deeds that affect only the relationship between man and God, and those that also have an effect on other human beings. There is no intrinsic difference between "Thou shall have no other God" and "Thou shall not murder." Both are divine commandments; the force of divine revelation is behind them both and justifies them both. Religious requirements and social ones cannot be separated, because both of them derive their authority from divine revelation, and both should be adhered to and obeyed for the same reason: the need to carry out God's commandment. The fact that the one can be justified on social grounds and grounds of self-interest, while the other cannot, does not affect their authority. Because of this, both the halakhah and Jewish ethics deal equally with the common themes of social ethics together with religious and ritualistic demands.

III

Talmudic-midrashic ethical literature, in the framework of the aggadah, probably reached its peak in the fifth and sixth centuries, but continued to develop for several centuries more, though not in the same innovative and forceful way. Midrashic collections were edited from various sources up to the fourteenth century, sometimes including material that cannot be found in earlier collections. A radical change in the literary and ideological matrix of Judaism occurred, however, in the tenth century and changed the position of Jewish ethics within it.

The unique characteristic of midrashic literature was its ability to include, within one literary genre, all the subjects of human literary and ideological creativity. The Midrash contains not only laws and ethical instructions, but also everything that was preserved by the ancient rabbis on subjects like history, geography, astronomy, narrative literature, hagiography, historiography, anthropology, and psychology, as well as exegesis, linguistics, and many other subjects. The normal separation of literary genres by their contents and literary form together was completely absent during the long centuries of talmudic-midrashic creativity, even though such distinctions were known and used by earlier Jewish writers, and can be found in biblical and post-biblical literature.

In the gaonic period (sixth to eleventh centuries) this unifying structure began to disintegrate. The first new, non-midrashic forms of expression are to be found in the realm of the halakhah: halakhic monographs and codes began to be written by the heads of the great academies of Jewish law in Babylonia, deviating from the previous talmudic-midrashic norm and presenting the halakhah in a literary form designed for the specific subject. This process gained momentum especially in the tenth century, when we find, for the first time since the period of the Mishnah in the first and second centuries C.E., books and treatises specifically dedicated to exegesis, language, biblical translations, polemical works, and halakhic monographs, and—among them—the first works dedicated specifically to philosophy and ethics. The central figure in this process was Rav Saadia Gaon (882-942), the head of the academy at Sura, whose many books and treatises laid the foundations for at least half a dozen literary subjects and genres.

Saadia's classic work of Jewish philosophy, *Emunot ve-Deot* ("The Book of Ideas and Beliefs"), includes as its tenth and last chapter a treatise which could have been written as a separate treatise on the subject of ethics: "On Human Behavior." This book, written in Arabic, marks the beginning of Jewish medieval ethical literature, and signifies the fact that ethics was separated from the vast body of the aggadah and Midrash and could be studied as a specific subject, expressed through its own literary vehicle.

Though there is no doubt that Jewish medieval ethics begins with Saadia's work, creativity in the earlier midrashic framework did not cease. Many midrashic collections, emphasizing ethics, were composed both in Saadia's lifetime and in the centuries after him. Creativity in the old manner continued to develop side by side with the new literary emphasis introduced by Saadia and his followers among the Jewish philosophers by dedicating specific works to it. It should be emphasized, therefore, that during the first centuries of the Middle Ages there existed concurrently Hebrew traditional ethical creativity in the form of midrashic collections, and the new way, begun by Saadia, based on the ideas of Greek philosophy which reached Jewish thinkers via the philosophical works of the Arabs.

One of the most important processes of the twelfth and thirteenth centuries in the realm of Jewish ethical creativity is the one in which new, original Jewish ethical works slowly but steadily gravitated toward the midrashic-aggadic literary form. This process, and its ideological and historical reasons, will be described in chapter 2, because most of the writers who participated in it belonged to the first groups of Jewish mystics in medieval Europe.

It can be stated that the two centuries (tenth to twelfth) in which Jewish ethics were expressed in treatises written in Arabic and governed by the logical and scientific categories of Greek philosophy were nothing but an interlude in the two-thousand-year history of Jewish ethics. If we view this period as a whole, looking at its broadest outlines, it becomes evident that medieval Hebrew ethical literature is the direct inheritor and continuation of the talmudic-midrashic aggadah. While all other subjects acquired their own literary genres in the Middle Ages, ethical ideas were expressed in literary forms close or identical to those of the aggadah and Midrash, very often in the literary genres of anthologies of rabbinic sayings or—more frequently—in collections of homilies that followed classical midrashic patterns.

This is one of the sources of the power of Hebrew ethical literature: its traditional nature, apparent in its close ties with ancient aggadah, and its ability to absorb and sustain conflicting ideas and attitudes. Just as in the classical Midrash one can hardly find an idea without a contradictory saying not far away, so medieval and early modern ethical literature was not required to represent and conform to one strict ideological system. The ancient openness of the aggadah gave its medieval inheritors who created Hebrew ethical literature the ability to use terminology derived from all schools of thought, to present systems built from fragments of various ideologies and to disregard contradictions, real or apparent, and to do all this with an aura of traditional authority. The connection with classical aggadah made Hebrew ethical literature a central power in medieval Jewish thought and everyday life.

IV

The attitude of medieval thinkers toward the aggadah should be taken into account when we assess the impact of Hebrew ethical literature. Modern scholars who study the ancient talmudic and midrashic ideas often reveal influences which contributed to the emergence of many midrashic sayings. Some are derived from the influence of Greek philosophy and ethics, and others from Persian and even Christian and gnostic ideology. But external influences are not the only source of conflicts of ideological divergence and contradictions in the aggadic sayings. There were different trends and schools among the ancient sages themselves—messianic and antimessianic, traditionalists and innovators, and many others. All were integrated into one body of thought, at least externally, and included in the midrashic collections. While modern scholarship can distinguish between conflicting schools and attitudes within talmudic literature, medieval scholars accepted it as one whole, in which every contradiction should be regarded as more apparent than real. The ingenuity of a medieval scholar can be judged, according to the standards of those days, by his ability to show the underlying harmony among the seemingly conflicting ideas and utterances. This fact may have set the tone for subsequent developments in medieval ethical literature, while it also accepted in harmony the products of the most divergent and conflicting theological schools.

One of the constant characteristics of Hebrew ethical works is their insistence on presenting ethical ideas as directly resulting from the correct interpretation of biblical verses and talmudic and midrashic sayings. While in philosophical works a writer may rely on logic and experience, in ethical works everything has to be proven by citing and interpreting an ancient text, even though the ethical considerations and the reasoning that led to the presented conclusion are clearly emphasized. This is the main characteristic of the Midrash, which relies on the biblical verse concerning every idea expressed in it; it is also the most prominent characteristic of Hebrew homiletics and sermons throughout the ages, and this is also a basic requirement of Hebrew ethical literature. Even philosophers who relied on Aristotelian logic as proof and basis for their conclusions, wrote popular ethical and homiletical literature using the traditional forms of exegesis and hermeneutics of biblical verses and talmudic sayings. A case in point is the great thirteenth-century rationalist of the court of Emperor Frederick II, Rabbi Jacob Anatoli, whose philosophical work on the subject of ethics, *Malemad ha-Talmidim*, is written in the form of a series of sermons, in the traditional manner, on portions of the Torah.

This continuity through a vast literature written from the time of the Second Commonwealth to the twentieth century, and its consistency in every geographic region in which Jews lived in ancient, medieval, and modern times, made Jewish ethics a formidable treasury in which every idea, traditional or radical, revolutionary or conservative, originally Jewish or derived from an external source, could find a place, provided it was expressed in the traditional literary form of this literature and produced as proof biblical texts and talmudic sayings. No boundaries were set to the manner in which the connection between the idea and the text could be proven. It need not be logical or literal; midrashic interpretations of verses seldom follow logic or the literal meaning. It even became one of the main aesthetic elements of this literature: to produce a surprising, elegant, and novel connection between the ancient text and the modern idea expressed in the work. As long as the basic norm was preserved—that every notion presented in the work is derived (even in the most far-fetched manner) from the ancient text—everything was permissible and the minimum requirements were regarded as fulfilled. Even when books containing the same ideology were criticized or even banned, ethical literature continued to flourish unhindered.

V

Jewish mysticism and Jewish ethics met, for the first time, in the last years of the twelfth century and the first half of the thirteenth. The process of this meeting and the subsequent, lasting impact that this meeting had on the nature of Jewish ethics and—through ethical literature—on Jewish society and history, will be discussed in some detail in the chapters that follow. It should be stressed, however, that both Jewish mysticism and Jewish ethics developed for many centuries, or even a millennium and more, before this meeting occurred in southern and central Europe of the Middle Ages.

The first groups of Jewish mystics who produced a mystical literature that survived as a separate body of mystical lore are known as the Hekhalot ("Divine Palaces") and Merkabah ("Holy Chariot") mystics of the talmudic period. Their systems were developed from the times of the ancient sages of the second century C.E., up to the gaonic period in the early Middle Ages. More than a score of their mystical and magical works were preserved. These dealt with the secrets revealed to Ezekiel in his vision of the chariot, with mystical means of acquiring esoteric knowledge, and especially with the process of the "descent to the chariot"—the mystical uplifting from one divine palace to the next until the mystic reaches the seventh and supreme palace, where the enormous figure of the Creator (described in anthropomorphic terms in the text *Shiur Komah*, "The Measurement of Their Height") is sitting on its throne surrounded by the archangels, headed by the mysterious Metatron, "the Prince of the Face."[4]

This mystical literature, most diverse in its subjects (which include also cosmogony and cosmology), does not deal with ethics at all. It seems that the practical side of religious life was not regarded as an integral part of mystical speculation. It is not that these mystics disregarded religious perfection in the fields of law and ethics; they apparently took it for granted that mysticism begins when these basic perfections have already been reached. Several times in these texts we find brief descriptions of the mystic as perfect in every earthly and religious way, as well as being morally superior to the common man. But no details are given, and no directions are offered concerning the ways that these perfections are to be achieved. Mysticism and ethics are regarded as separate and independent realms; only one who is perfect in every other way is viewed as a candidate for mystical instruction and achievement.

While nineteenth-century scholars treated Hekhalot and Merkabah mysticism as a late phenomenon that does not belong to the intellectual world of the Talmud and the Midrash, contemporary scholarship, following the discoveries and the analyses of Gershom Scholem and Saul Lieberman, views these mystical texts as developing within the same world in which the Talmud and Midrash were created. There are many parallels between them, and quite a few talmudic and midrashic passages cannot be understood if one does not take into account their ideological background revealed in the Hekhalot texts. However, these talmudic and midrashic texts usually have nothing to do with ethics, but deal with cosmology, revelation, and theology. It seems that the early Jewish mystics of ancient times did not see fit to draw specific ethical conclusions from the esoteric secrets revealed to them in a mystical manner. Thus, for over a millennium we observe a parallel development of Jewish ethics on the one side and Jewish mysticism on the other without the two merging to produce a mystical system of ethics. This changed in the Middle Ages, and the process of this change is described in chapter 2.

VI

A final note is needed concerning the meaning of the term "ethics" in this context. When describing biblical ethics we usually mean those practical and behavioral demands presented by God which are not strictly legal, ritualistic, or social demands. Advice concerning the everyday way of life, instruction in abstaining from evil, and the pursuit of perfection in attitude and deed are regarded as ethical; these are usually presented in the Bible in the most concrete and practical terms. The verses frequently present the ethical demands without an explanation of the ideological background, which sometimes can be surmised and very often is hidden.

Talmudic and midrashic ethics are much more explicit both in the concrete details of the desired pattern of behavior and the rationale behind these demands. There is an overall balance in this vast literature between the exposition of the moral way of life and the abstract descriptions of good and evil, though the emphasis is still on the practical, concrete instructions. The dividing line between law and ethics is very thin, and sometimes nearly impossible to draw, as explained above. Ethical considerations, for instance, usually serve as a reason for a legal decision. The way the halakhah is formulated can often reveal the ethical preferences of the legal authorities who wrote and explained its demands. Still, the practical side is paramount here also, and the theory is, at best, briefly and succinctly hinted at.

Medieval Judaism received from its ancient, revered sacred books of the Bible and Talmud a most detailed description of the ethical way of life to be followed by a Jew who wishes to achieve ethical perfection as a religious requirement. A thorough study of the Talmud and Midrash was regarded as answering all the practical questions that a Jew might face in his search for the moral way in which to behave, both toward his Creator and toward his fellow men. The system, however, was far from complete concerning the reasons why a man should do this and not that, what is the abstract guideline and the theological basis of the choice of one set of actions over the other. There was the obvious traditionalistic answer to every inquiry concerning the reasons: this is what is demanded by God, as proven by the text of the biblical verses as interpreted homiletically by the sages of the Talmud and Midrash. The source of authority, therefore, was the ancient revelation of God to Moses and the people of Israel on Mount Sinai, when the Torah was given, and all ethical (as well as legal) decisions are derived from the correct understanding of the contents of that divine revelation. Medieval Jewish ethics are based on the feeling that this answer is insufficient.

Taken as a whole, medieval and early modern Hebrew ethical literature presents very few new ways of behaving and practical instructions that cannot be found in biblical and talmudic sources. There are many exceptions to this generalization, and several of the great teachers of Jewish ethics, most notably Rabbi Judah the Pious of Regensburg, presented whole systems of practical instruction that are new in character. But the main subject of Hebrew ethics in this period is not what to do, but why to do it, when the practical instructions are those derived from the ancient sources.

In the Middle Ages Jewish ethical systems differ from each other according to the theological school they represent—philosophical, mystical, rabbinic, or Ashkenazi Hasidic—and not in the system of practical instructions demanded by them. Most ethical demands are taken for granted, and presented in a definitive form in the talmudic and midrashic texts, usually without argument concerning their necessity or concerning the details of their performance. The discussion, the conflicts, and the arguments usually concern the underlying reason and the place that these actions have in the totality of the image of religious perfection. The details of this process, which moved the emphasis in Jewish ethics from the "what" to the "why," from actions to ethical values, and therefore from the practical to the abstract, from the material to the spiritual realm in religious life, are the subject of the analysis that follows.

2

PHILOSOPHICAL ETHICS
AND THE EARLY KABBALISTS

I

FOUR MAIN STAGES can be identified in the history of Jewish ethical
thought in the Middle Ages, between the tenth and the seventeenth centuries. The first stage is the emergence of Jewish philosophical, rationalistic ethics, which is combined with the appearance of rationalistic philosophy as a dominant school among
Jewish rabbis and intellectuals in the Near East and southern
Europe from the tenth century onward. The early Jewish philosophers of the Middle Ages wrote their works in Arabic, and
their ethical systems were presented in the same language, as a part
of their presentation of the totality of their rationalistic world
views. These philosophers expressed their conceptions of ethics
either in chapters dedicated to moral behavior in their comprehensive philosophical works, or in separate ethical treatises and books,
usually written in the same style and governed by the same logical
maxims as their other philosophical works. Their aim was to re-
formulate and re-present the essence of Jewish religion and theology according to the new philosophical ideas which they received
from the dominant Moslem culture around them, which in turn
was based to a very large extent on the re-emergence of Greek
philosophy in an Arab garb. The Arab philosophers included in
their works ancient Greek philosophical texts and ideas and interpreted them; many texts were translated from Greek to Arabic, and

others adopted in various ways. The Jewish philosophers, who were a part of Arab civilization, were thus able to come into touch, for the first time, with the full power of Greek philosophical thought. Jewish rationalistic ethics was developed in this atmosphere of Moslem intellectual tolerance, Arabic culture, and the impact of Greek philosophy on the ancient traditions of biblical and talmudic Judaism.[1]

The second stage of the development of Jewish ethics in the Middle Ages begins with the spread of Jewish rationalistic philosophy and ethics beyond the boundaries of Arabic-speaking countries in the Near East, North Africa, and Spain. Its influence reached steadily north, from southern Spain to Catalonia and Provence, and then to Italy. Jewish communities in these areas were aware that novel concepts had emerged and were employed by Jewish thinkers, but were unable to participate in this movement because they could not read the works of the Jewish philosophers in the Arabic original. They sought Hebrew translations of the Arabic works, or similar works written originally in Hebrew. Some Jewish philosophers who traveled outside the Arabic sphere of culture were aware of these needs, and in the twelfth century Hebrew philosophical and ethical-philosophical literature begins to emerge. Rabbi Judah Ibn Tibbon began his great project, continued by his descendants, of translating the main Jewish philosophical books into Hebrew,[2] and philosophers like Abraham Ibn Ezra and Abraham bar Hijja[3] began to write philosophical and ethical works in Hebrew, for the benefit of the Jewish communities in Christian Europe.

This second stage is, therefore, that of the transformation of Jewish rationalistic ethics from being a part of Judeo-Arabic culture into a genre of Hebrew literature. This transition was not a purely technical one of translation from one language to another, because the works written in Hebrew acquired the characteristics of traditional Hebrew ethics even though they presented ideas and concepts based on Greek and Arabic philosophy.

The third stage began early in the thirteenth century, when, for the first time in medieval southern Europe, treatises on ethics began to be written in Hebrew without any philosophical background, expounding Jewish traditional ethics based on the Talmud and Midrash. This literature developed continuously from the early thirteenth century for many centuries, and is often called by the somewhat uninformative appellation "rabbinic ethical literature." For three centuries this literature developed side by side with rationalistic philosophical ethical literature in Hebrew, but gained increasing popularity at the expense of philosophical ethical literature.[4] The beginning of this third stage in the history of Jewish ethics, and its relationship with Jewish mysticism, which began to develop shortly before this period in southern Europe, is the subject of this chapter.

The fourth stage followed directly from the previous one: the appearance of Jewish mystical ethics, based in many cases on works of "rabbinic ethics." Sometimes it is very difficult, for reasons which will be discussed below, to distinguish between "rabbinic" and mystical works in the field of ethics. Jewish mystical ethics, or kabbalistic ethics, did not reach its final stage of development until the sixteenth century, after the expulsion of the Jews from Spain in 1492. In that century, in the small town of Safed in Upper Galilee, kabbalistic ethical works began to be written in a systematic way and soon became one of the major forces shaping Jewish culture.[5] But the early mystics of the thirteenth to the fifteenth centuries hesitated to bring the teachings of the Kabbalah to the wide public, and, as ethical works by definition are dedicated to the education of the masses, they tended to hide the full extent of their mystical-ethical ideas when writing popular works. After the expulsion from Spain a major change occurred. The Kabbalah became a central power in Jewish culture, and thus began the period in which Jewish mystical ethics dominated Jewish ethical creativity.

Side by side with the beginning of the second and third stages, the appearance of Hebrew philosophical works of ethics in the twelfth century and the beginning of "rabbinic" ethical literature in the thirteenth century, another major phenomenon occurred:

the creation of Ashkenazi Hasidic ethics by the Jewish pietistic and mystical movement, Ashkenazi Hasidism, in the twelfth and thirteenth centuries in central Europe, mainly in Germany. This movement, which was based on an esoteric theological tradition containing mystical elements, created systems of ethics which at first had a profound influence on Jewish ethics in central Europe, but later merged with the ethical systems of the kabbalists and shaped the norms of late medieval and early modern Jewish ethics as a whole.[6]

The theological background of the appearance of Jewish philosophical ethics in Arabic and Hebrew—the first and second stages described above—is quite clear: the development of Jewish philosophy under the influence of Arab civilization and the systematic study of the ancient sources of Greek philosophy and their adaptation to the needs of Jewish religious thought. But the background for the last two stages and that of the Ashkenazi Hasidic ethical system is much less clear. It is my intention to investigate both the background of the emergence of these trends and the reasons for it, and to point out the role of Jewish mysticism in shaping Jewish ethics in the Middle Ages and early modern times.

II

The most outstanding characteristic of the way Jewish rationalistic philosophers in the Middle Ages presented their systematic treatments of the subject of ethics is that they discussed it as if it were a completely new aspect in Jewish culture and religion, as if their presentation was the original discovery of the subject. Ancient Jewish literature really did not contain theological treatises, and a medieval philosopher writing such a work had every right to feel that he was presenting his readers with something never before done in Jewish religious thought. But in the realm of ethics the situation is quite different. Biblical literature as well as post-biblical, talmudic, and midrashic literature did contain works dedicated to ethical norms and detailed instruction. Throughout Jewish religious literature in the ancient period, the question of the right way for man to live, behave, and worship his God is a paramount one, shaping to a large extent most of the Hebrew works written at that time.

The fact that the Jewish philosophers of the tenth and eleventh centuries all but ignored this enormous heritage and started dealing with Jewish ethics as if they were the first to present the subject had important consequences for later developments in this field, for naturally traditionalist thinkers reacted in their own way to this attitude apparent in the works of their philosophical antagonists.

This attitude appeared in the first half of the tenth century, with the philosophical work *Emunot ve-Deot* ("The Book of Beliefs and Ideas"), by Rav Saadia Gaon, written while the author was serving as the head of the great academy of Sura situated in Baghdad in Babylonia. Saadia devoted the tenth and last chapter in his comprehensive theological book to the problems of the right way for humans to behave. In that brief chapter he intended to present a systematic treatment of all ethical problems, organized around one cardinal principle.

His starting point contains theological, cosmological, and anthropological axioms. The first is that God created man and his psyche as one whole, containing thirteen inclinations or drives.[7] The list of these thirteen inclinations is most variegated, including the desire for food, sex, "rest" (i.e., sloth), longevity, and revenge, as well as for the study of the Torah and the worship of God. Saadia compared the creation of man to that of other beings, and stated that there can be nothing unnecessary or superfluous in God's work. Therefore, everything found within man must serve a good purpose. Just as a tree is comprised of diverse elements, such as a trunk, branches, roots, leaves, and so forth, each contributing harmoniously to its existence, all the inclinations found within man, excluding none, must be regarded as created by God and contributing to human existence. Ethics means, according to Saadia, the right way in which a man should utilize all these inclinations in a harmonious way and in the right proportions in order to fulfill God's intention in his creation. Most of this chapter by Saadia is dedicated to the demonstration that complete concentration on any one of the inclinations is bad, even if it is the worship of God or the study of the Torah. It is also wrong to neglect any of the inclinations, including lust or sloth, because each has its time and place if used in the right proportion. The ethical man has to construct his life in a measured, harmonious way so that all his drives will be used in the right balance, and thus he will be happy in his early life and fulfill God's intention in his creation: to produce a harmonious whole from variegated and even conflicting different parts.

It is interesting to note how Saadia explained what is wrong with concentration on the fulfillment of only one of the drives. According to his detailed explanations, such a concentration—be it on study or on revenge—causes disease or early death, or at least prevents man from fully enjoying life. The correct balance is "good" because it enables man to enjoy long and healthy life. The system presented by Saadia attempts to be a systematic, scientific one and is oriented completely to secular, even hedonistic, happiness.

In this chapter Saadia quoted many biblical verses and some talmudic sayings in order to illustrate and strengthen his statements. Yet the ancient, traditional sources do not serve as a basis for shaping his systematic presentation; he could have arrived at his conclusions and presented them clearly without the support of his carefully selected biblical examples. This tenth chapter in his theological work, which may have been written as a separate and independent treatise, is presented as a new beginning, a first presentation of Jewish ethics, as if nothing had been said on the subject within Judaism before him. If this is the case in an ethical work written by the leading rabbinic scholar and halakhist of his time, the great leader of traditional Judaism whose center was the academy of Sura, one can imagine what picture will emerge from

the works of writers more deeply involved in the study of philosophy and less immersed in rabbinic tradition than Saadia.

The philosophical approach to ethics found in Saadia's treatment
of the subject was developed further by the great philosopher and
poet, Rabbi Solomon Ibn Gabirol, in his brief ethical treatise
Tikkun Midot ha-Nefesh ("The Correction of the Soul's Inclinations").[8] In this book Ibn Gabirol attempted to give a physiological
basis to ethical preferences. He presented a table of twenty human
inclinations and ethical values, divided into ten pairs of conflicting
ones, like pride and humility, and arranged in five groups, two
pairs in each. Each of these groups was connected with one of the
five senses—pride with the sense of sight, or anger with the sense
of smell. The four inclinations in each such group correspond,
according to this system, to the four elements of creation (air, fire,
water, earth) and to the four fluids in the human body. Thus, each
inclination reflects the character of one of the elements and one of
the fluids: anger, for example, is the reflection of the element of fire
and the red *mara*, and works through one of the five senses, smell.
Its characteristics, as well as its ethical value, are decided by this
natural, physiological combination. Ethical behavior, therefore,
should be studied and treated according to purely scientific, physical criteria. Ethics should not be regarded as a part of theology or
philosophy, but rather as one of the physical sciences.

Ibn Gabirol used over a hundred biblical verses in this brief
treatise, and these verses do serve an important role in the con-
struction of his system, though in a most unusual way. The verses
were used in order to create a connection—often quite an artificial
one—between the ethical value discussed and the particular sense
with which Ibn Gabirol wished to link it. Anger, for instance, is
connected with the sense of smell because biblical imagery associates it with the nose, in descriptions of both human and divine
anger.[9] Pride is connected with the sense of sight because of some
biblical verses which describe the effects of pride on the eyes. Ibn
Gabirol is revealed here as a homiletical writer, who shows how the

Bible associates the twenty inclinations with various limbs and
senses, and transfers this to the scheme of relationship between
ethical values and the five senses. This is a completely arbitrary
system, in which scientific presentation is based on homiletical
treatment of biblical verses.[10]

The ethical system presented in this treatise is regarded by the
author as an entirely new departure, which does not rely on any
previous Jewish conception of ethics. Ibn Gabirol, like Saadia,
believes that the new scientific horizons opened before Jewish
writers in the Middle Ages necessitate a novel approach, which
would disregard the ancient past and use quotations from biblical
and talmudic sources only to illustrate or strengthen, by homiletical means, the new system.

The same phonomenon, though in a different guise, is to be
found in the most important and influential work of Jewish philosophical ethics: Rabbi Bahya Ibn Paquda's *Hovot ha-Levavot* ("The
Duties of the Heart"), probably written in the eleventh century in
southern Spain.[11] This work represents a new approach in Jewish
ethics in a most profound and far-reaching manner.

While Solomon Ibn Gabirol sought the basis of ethical behavior
in human physiology, Rabbi Bahya sought the exact opposite: to
define a Jewish system of religious and ethical behavior that is
completely spiritual and does not touch any of man's limbs or
senses. In the introduction to his book he complained that while
God created man as a dual creature, comprised of a soul and a body,
the Jewish legal and ethical works that had been written before him
concentrated exclusively on the body, neglecting to deal with the
spiritual part of man and with spiritual commandments and
norms. Volumes were written, according to him, on what man
should do, while hardly a treatise existed that described what he
should feel and believe in. In order to supply this missing dimension in Jewish ethics, which Bahya regarded as the most essential
for religious life, he constructed in the "Duties of the Heart" a
system of ten basic spiritual "duties" or "commandments," which
he suggested should be central in a Jew's religious life. They are

recognized by their complete independence of any physical or sensual element. They include such "duties" as the knowledge of God's unity, the intellectual examination of God's work in the creation of the world, self-examination of one's soul, repentance, the fear and love of God, and others. He did not include such "spiritual" elements of religious life as prayer or the study of the Torah, because of their connection with the body and the senses.[12] He was seeking a completely spiritual system, independent of any contact with the physical part of man.

Bahya contradicted the basic attitudes of Saadia and Ibn Gabirol by presenting a deeply religious and spiritual ethical system as a basis of religious life. Yet he does conform to the same tendency found in their works, by viewing his book on Jewish ethics as the "first," as a completely new departure, disregarding the vast literature on the subject that preceded him. There is a deep feeling of assuming a great task in the way the book was written, as if Bahya believed that he was the first Jewish thinker who understood the true character of Judaism and his book was the first presentation of this truth. Like Saadia and Ibn Gabirol, Bahya also used many biblical quotations (besides hundreds of quotations from non-Jewish sources), but they are intended only to support his system, and not as a dominant element that can dictate its views to the medieval moralist.

In many respects Bahya's ethics can be regarded as the most radical and revolutionary in Jewish ethical-philosophical literature. When discussing the "duties of the limbs," in contradistinction to the "duties of the heart," he clearly states that their performance does not include any religious value if they are not coupled, at least, with a spiritual "intention" which gives them value. When they are performed with such an intention (*kavvanah*), the source of their meaning is the spiritual intention and not the deed itself. As the "duties of the limbs" include all the traditional commandments, precepts, and ethical, social, and ritualistic demands of Judaism, Bahya in fact denies the existence of an intrinsic religious value in the performance of the basic Jewish rituals, such as prayers and the observation of the Sabbath and the holy days, and social commandments, such as charity. They may have some value only if a spiritual experience accompanies them, but this spiritual experience does not have to be coupled with the physical deed. It is even more perfect if it stands alone, without any connection with the physical or the sensual parts of man, and then it becomes a "duty of the heart," the supreme element of religious life.

As Jewish life is totally dependent on the performance of the physical commandments, Bahya's book could very easily be regarded as heretical, preaching the secondary status—if any—of everything that was regarded as of paramount importance in Judaism. It should be noted that this did not happen. Bahya was never declared a heretic; his work was never, as far as we know, criticized by subsequent generations. It was translated from the Arabic into Hebrew in the second half of the twelfth century by Rabbi Judah Ibn Tibbon, [13] who also translated Saadia's and Ibn Gabirol's works. "The Duties of the Heart" in Hebrew was universally accepted by later Jewish writers as a work of profound piety and deep religious expression. Bahya is called in later ethical literature "the Hasid," the pious, a title given only to a very few eminent spiritualists in the Middle Ages (two of whom—Rabbi Isaac the Blind and Rabbi Judah the Pious of Regensburg—will be discussed below). Even when Jewish philosophy was completely discredited in the sixteenth century and later, *The Duties of the Heart* was still quoted and relied upon by almost all ethical writers. The most important ethical work of mystical ethics writtenn in sixteenth century Safed—*Reshit Hochmah* ("The Beginnings of Wisdom") by Rabbi Eliyahu de Vidas—includes extensive quotations from Bahya's work, all presented with great respect, as if the author were a great kabbalist. [14] The same phenomenon is apparent in all later kabbalistic ethical literature, up to and including modern Hasidic homiletical works. When the modern writer, S. Y. Agnon, in his first novel, *The Bridal Canopy*, wished to portray a nineteenth-century Jewish orthodoxy, he put into the mouth of his representative hero quotations from "the Hasid, the author of *Hovot ha-Levavot*."[15]

The Duties of the Heart thus became a classic of Jewish ethics, accepted by philosophers and pietists, kabbalists and traditionalists alike, without even a hint of controversy or criticism. It seems that we have here one of the clearest demonstrations of the power of Hebrew ethical literature to absorb the most radical ideas and incorporate them into the totality of Jewish ethical tradition.

A fourth work should be added to the list of philosophical ethical treatises written in Arabic in twelfth-century Spain and Egypt and presenting an ethical system as if the subject were new: Moses Maimonides' *Shemonah Peraqim* ("Eight Chapters"), his introduction to the commentary on the tractate *Avot* of the Mishnah, a tractate dedicated mainly to ethics.[16] Even though Maimonides intends to interpret classical talmudic ethics in this introduction, his brief treatise is presented as an original system of ethics, beginning neither with physiology, like Ibn Gabirol, nor with spiritualization, like Bahya, but with a brief description of human psychology, which for him serves as a scientific basis for ethical teaching. Maimonides does quote several talmudic sayings in this book and analyzes them, but only in order to prove that there is no contradiction between the system he presents and the meaning of these sayings. Maimonides, the greatest Jewish philosopher of the Middle Ages, can hardly be categorized, and his works usually are exceptions to any generalization; yet the basic trend to present philosophical ethics as if there was no precedent to a systematic discussion of the subject is apparent in "Eight Chapters" no less than in the previous works of this genre.

III

In the twelfth century, some Jewish philosophers who were familiar with the cultural situation of Jewish communities in

Christian Europe, began to write ethical-philosophical treatises in Hebrew, in order to enable those communities, which did not belong to the sphere of Arabic-speaking civilization, to be acquainted with the new approach toward ethics presented by the Arabic-writing philosophers. The most important work of this sort is Rabbi Abraham bar Hijja's collection of four sermons, probably delivered on the High Holy Days, and dealing mainly with the subject of repentance— *Hegyon ha-Nefesh*. [17] From a literary point of view, bar Hijja's work is radically different from those of the Arabic-writing philosophers. Bar Hijja used classical techniques of Hebrew homiletics found in the Midrash, and to some extent structured his book in a traditional manner. Yet the basic approach to ethics found in previous philosophical works in this field is present in this Hebrew work as well.

In the opening paragraphs of *Hegyon ha-Nefesh*, Rabbi bar Hijja presented a comprehensive medieval philosophical description of the process of creation, based mainly on neo-Platonic philosophy of the time; he refers to his non-Jewish philosophical sources as "*Hachmey ha-Mechkar*," "the wise scientists" or "philosophers." This detailed discussion of the creation does not contain any reference to a biblical or other Jewish source or even a Jewish concept. But after completing this presentation bar Hijja states that properly interpreted, the first chapters of the book of Genesis present exactly the same picture. He proves this by a detailed homiletical exegesis of the key terms in these chapters, presenting the Hebrew biblical words as exact equivalents of the basic philosophical terms used to explain the process of creation (for instance: *tohu* and *bohu* are equivalents of the philosophical "matter" and "form"). [18]

Bar Hijja followed the same method throughout the work, relying heavily on neo-Platonic concepts, but translating them into Hebrew traditional terms and demonstrating by homiletical means the basic identity that he believed existed between the two systems. Bar Hijja's book is the first Hebrew homiletical work written in Europe, and the first Hebrew independent work dedicated to the subject of repentance. It contains many more traditional Jewish concepts and ideas than works written in Arabic, but his ethical system is based on non-Jewish philosophy and derives its power and its authority from these sources. Bar Hijja probably regarded his work as revealing the underlying identity between philosophical views and the content of Jewish tradition, and in that sense he, too, presented a new departure, the opening of a new era in Jewish ethical thought. The sense of historical continuity between the old Jewish classics and the new philosophical systems is completely lacking in *Hegyon ha-Nefesh*; rather, philosophy is the underlying meaning of rabbinic ethics.

To a lesser extent, the same can be said concerning the second Hebrew treatise on ethics written in the twelfth century, Rabbi Abraham Ibn Ezra's *Yesod Mora* ("The Foundation of the Fear of God").[19] This short treatise contains several sections taken from the author's monumental commentary on the Bible. Ibn Ezra suggests a systematic organization of the traditional Jewish *mitzvot*, commandments, according to the accepted logical categories of classification. The ethical ideas presented are not developed into a complete and comprehensive system of ethics. His statements rely heavily on the new distinctions introduced by him, which are derived from medieval logic. Previous Jewish concepts do not serve as a dominant and meaningful source, and are quoted mainly to strengthen ideas derived from other sources.

A third twelfth-century work in this field, unique in many ways, is Moses Maimonides' *Sefer ha-Mada*, especially the section "Hilchot Deot" (Ethical Norms). This book is the first among the fourteen books of Maimonides' classical work in Jewish law, the greatest Hebrew work of codification in the Middle Ages. *Sefer ha-Mada*[20] is dedicated to a legal presentation of the demands of Judaism in the realm of ideas and beliefs, ethical values, daily behavior, and social customs. Maimonides used in this book the language and style of the Mishnah, presenting an "ethical code" that consists of a rewriting and editing, according to his views, of the talmudic and midrashic material on the subject.

This work is entirely different from the others discussed above, because it intends to present, or re-present, classical Jewish ethics in a formal, legalistic way. It is a work of ethics even though it is aimed to be, rather, a code of law that, according to Maimonides, is comprehensive and should cover all aspects of human life. It is an exception, created under unique circumstances, but its impact on subsequent Jewish works in the field of ethics was considerable and sometimes decisive.

By the end of the twelfth century, Judaism had created a distinct ethical school, that of the Jewish philosophers, most of them writing in Arabic although some beginnings in Hebrew were already present. This school of Jewish ethics was immensely popular and influential, especially as it was the only one in the sphere of influence of Arabic culture and in southern Europe adjacent to it. The authors of these works believed that they were bringing into Jewish thought a system of new ideas, based on scientific investigation of cosmology, theology, or psychology, and their source of authority was the deductive logic of medieval philosophy. Jewish traditional expressions on the subject of ethics were treated as secondary, supportive at best. It is not surprising that thirteenth-century Jewish traditionalists reacted to this challenge and presented an altogether different system of Jewish ethics in which mysticism often replaced philosophy.

IV

Hebrew nonphilosophical, or "rabbinic," ethical literature of the first half of the thirteenth century reflects a different attitude toward traditional Jewish ethics when compared to the ethical works of the Jewish philosophers. In this literature, traditional ethics, especially talmudic and midrashic ethical sources, are the dominant element, sometimes to the exclusion of any other source. The authors of these works of ethics do not only rely on the ancient sources to strengthen and prove their ideas; very often the talmudic sayings themselves *are* their ideas. Chapters and sections in these works can be read as anthologies of rabbinic sayings on the subject under discussion. Medieval terminology is often avoided, while the traditional talmudic terms serve as the basis of the presentation of ethical values. There are only a few attempts to "modernize" the ancient sources. It is as if the authors were saying that no contemporary writer can put these ideas into words better than did the ancient sages of the Talmud and Midrash.

The first writers who demonstrated this new attitude toward traditional ethical sources in the first half of the thirteenth century in Spain were:

1. Rabbi Moses ben Nachman, the famous Nachmanides, author of the great commentary on the Pentateuch, a great authority in the halakhah, and the leader of Spanish Jewry at that time;[21]

2. Nachmanides' nephew, Rabbi Jonah Gerondi, whose commentaries on the book of Proverbs and the tractate *Avot* are the first in the new genre of ethical commentaries on ancient books. He is famous in the history of Jewish thought especially because of his ethical work, *Shaarey Teshuvah* ("The Gates of Repentance"), which became a landmark in the history of Hebrew ethical literature;[22]

3. Rabbi Jacob ben Sheshet, author of the profound ethical book *Ha-Emunah veha-Bitahon* ("Faith and Trust"), as well as several other works;[23]

4. Rabbi Asher ben David, author of the little known ethical work *Perush Yud-Gimel Midot* ("Commentary on the Thirteen Ethical Attributes").[24]

Though there is a general similarity among them, these four authors do not treat their subject in an identical manner. Nachmanides used the traditional, talmudic-midrashic material extensively in his *Torat ha-Adam* ("The Law of Man"), especially in its last section, "Shaar ha-Gemul" ("The Gate of Retribution"), where his exposition of the various Jewish interpretations of eschatological retribution, both after death and in messianic times, is based almost exclusively on the presentation and exegesis of the

talmudic-midrashic sources. To a lesser degree we find the same
attitude in Nachmanides' sermons, where the problems he raises
are discussed in detail on the basis of the ancient sources.

Rabbi Jonah Gerondi's *Shaarey Teshuvah* is very close to the
anthological model, though to a different extent in the various
chapters of this book. He arranged all the talmudic material
concerning sin and penitence according to a systematic sequence,
so that the ancient traditions could speak for themselves and
answer the contemporary problems concerning repentance as raised
by the Jewish philosophers.

Rabbi Jacob ben Sheshet and Rabbi Asher ben David used
explicit kabbalistic symbolism in their treatment of the ethical
subjects presented in their works, but their treatises are constructed mainly around collections of talmudic and midrashic
sayings on ethical subjects.

These four authors, when compared to rationalistic writers of the
preceding centuries, present a common new attitude, which is in
sharp contrast with the philosophical expositions of Jewish ethics
from Saadia to Ibn Ezra. Nowhere in these works do we have the
feeling that the author presents us with an original approach, a
breakthrough in this subject. The picture they portray is one of
direct continuation, without any break or change. The ancient
sources are presented as completely relevant and as containing the
full answers to contemporary problems.

The ethical works of these four writers confront us with a
historically meaningful problem. After two and a half centuries in
which rationalistic philosophy was dominant in Jewish discussions
of ethics, in works which were designed to renew and even revolutionize Jewish conceptions of moralistic behavior along scientific
and spiritual lines, we suddenly find a wholly different attitude in a
significant body of ethical works. These works had a profound
impact on the development of Jewish ethics in the next three
centuries, so that we may conclude that they reflected an existing
need within Jewish thought of the Middle Ages. We must, therefore, inquire why and how this sudden change occurred.

V

The appearance of four writers whose works were written during the same two decades, who share the same attitude toward the ancient ethical traditions of Judaism, and who together contradict the previously accepted norms of philosophical ethics cannot be regarded as accidental. Even geography alone can prove the close connection among them: these four writers flourished and published in the small town of Gerona, in Catalonia, in northern Christian Spain. The possibility that four writers in one small town, in a Jewish community which at that time did not include more than a few hundred families,[25] reached independently the same conclusions concerning the desired nature of Hebrew ethical literature is very remote indeed. We must conclude that a new school of Jewish ethics emerged in Gerona about 1220-40.

What rules out the possibility of a coincidence is the fact that at least three of these four writers were well-known members of the small, esoteric Gerona school of kabbalists. Nachmanides was the leader of this school in this period, following in the footsteps of its founders, Rabbi Ezra ben Shlomo and Rabbi Azriel of Gerona.[26] The Gerona kabbalists received their mystical traditions from the first center of the Kabbalah in medieval Europe, the one that flourished in Provence at the end of the twelfth century and the beginning of the thirteenth. The teacher and leader of this school was Rabbi Isaac Sagi Nahor ("The Blind"),[27] son of the great halakhist and mystic, Rabbi Abraham ben David of Posquièrre. Rabbi Isaac the Blind was the author of the first kabbalistic treatise in the Middle Ages by a known writer, his commentary on *Sefer Yezirah* ("The Book of Creation," a cosmological and cosmogonical work describing the process of the creation, with some mystical elements, written in the talmudic period).[28] The first leaders of the Gerona school, Rabbi Ezra and Rabbi Azriel, were disciples of Rabbi Isaac the Blind.

Rabbi Jacob ben Sheshet, author of the ethical work Ha-Emunah veha-Bitahon, was the most prolific writer of the Gerona school, and among other things wrote a polemical answer to Rabbi Shmuel Ibn Tibbon (the philosopher and translator into Hebrew of Maimonides' *Guide for the Perplexed*), who wrote a commentary on the first chapters of Genesis in his philosophical work *Ma'amar Yiqavu ha-Mayim* ("Let the Waters Be Gathered").[29] Rabbi ben Sheshet in his answer, *Meshiv Devarim Nechochim* ("A Refutation"), attacked the philosophical bases of Ibn Tibbon's approach, on traditional and kabbalistic grounds. He also wrote an ethical treatise on the Ten Commandments, *Sha'ar ha-Shamayim* ("The Gate of Heaven"), in which he used kabbalistic terminology.[30]

The third kabbalist in this group was Rabbi Asher ben David, the author of *Perush Yud Gimel Middot*, the kabbalistic treatises on the Holy Name (*Perush Shem ha-Meforash*), and other brief kabbalistic treatises. Rabbi Asher was a nephew of Rabbi Isaac the Blind, who sent him to the kabbalists in Gerona for a specific reason as will be explained below.[31]

Did the fourth writer and the best known among them in ethical literature, Rabbi Jonah Gerondi, belong to this school of kabbalists? There are two basic facts relating to this problem, each leading to a different conclusion. On the one hand, in Rabbi Isaac the Blind's letter to the Gerona kabbalists the name "Jonah" appears; Rabbi Isaac the Blind addressed his letter to "Rabbi Moses and Rabbi Jonah," and G. Scholem, who published and analyzed it, reached the conclusion that these recipients were Rabbi Moses ben Nachman (Nachmanides) and his nephew, Rabbi Jonah Gerondi.[32] If so— and some other documents seem to support this possibility—Rabbi Jonah was one of the Gerona kabbalists, who had contacts in kabbalistic matters with the great teacher, Rabbi Isaac, in Provence.

On the other hand, we have at least three books and several short treatises by Rabbi Jonah, none of which includes any reference to kabbalistic symbolism. From the books themselves we would never even try to connect Rabbi Jonah Gerondi with the Kabbalah. His ideas and expositions are purely traditional, without any clear hint of another, more recent, ideology to support them, such as we can find in the works of the other three ethical writers in Gerona.

There are only two possible ways of resolving this contradiction. One is to surmise that there was in Gerona another kabbalist by the name of Jonah, who was also close to Nachmanides, and that it is he who was mentioned by Rabbi Isaac the Blind. The other possibility is that Rabbi Jonah systematically and successfully hid his kabbalist attitudes and kept them out of his published works in the field of ethics. Which of these two possibilities is more probable?

In order to answer this question we must turn to the actual content of the letter by Rabbi Isaac the Blind to the Gerona kabbalists. Gershom Scholem discovered this letter and published it fifty years ago, and it served then, as it does now, as one of the most important documents for the understanding of the historical development of the Kabbalah in Europe, in Provence and Gerona.[33] The main purpose of the letter was to express Rabbi Isaac's anger when he heard that his disciples in Gerona did not keep their kabbalistic traditions secret, but talked about them openly and published books on mystical subjects. Rabbi Isaac believed that there was great danger of misunderstanding if the Kabbalah were revealed to the uninitiated, and that kabbalistic secrets should not even be put on paper in the form of a book. He stated in this letter: "A written book cannot be hidden in any cupboard,"[34] and insisted that the Gerona mystics immediately stop this practice.

Scholem suggested, when he analyzed this letter, that Rabbi Isaac was referring to Rabbi Ezra ben Shlomo and Rabbi Azriel. These two early kabbalists in Gerona did indeed write several kabbalistic works, commentaries on biblical books (*The Song of Songs*, by Rabbi Ezra), on talmudic aggadot, and on the prayers.[35] It seems that these books angered the old master very much and caused him to write this letter. If so, he was undoubtedly successful: the later kabbalists in Gerona did not write mystical works, as did their predecessors.

Another point in Rabbi Isaac's letter is his reference to an invitation he received from Gerona to visit the kabbalist center there. Rabbi Isaac answered that he could not undertake the hardships of such travel at his age and in failing health, but instead he was sending to Gerona his nephew, Rabbi Asher ben David, who would teach the Gerona kabbalists whatever they needed to know.[36] Rabbi Asher was, therefore, an emissary from Provence to Gerona, whom Rabbi Isaac appointed to be his representative, asking the Spanish kabbalists to accept his authority as they would accept that of Rabbi Isaac himself.

When we analyze the works of Rabbi Asher ben David, it is indeed apparent that he writes as an emissary and a representative. We have a brief commentary attributed to him in two manuscripts on the first chapter of Genesis—the same text also appearing elsewhere as the work of another unknown person, Rabbi Joseph ben Shmuel.[37] It seems that the treatise was indeed one of Rabbi Isaac the Blind's traditions, which was reported to the kabbalists in Spain from two sources. Rabbi Asher's introduction to his collection of works, *Sefer ha-Yihhud* ("The Book of Divine Unity"), contains expressions that bear the characteristics of an emissary, away from his own place, speaking to the people to whom he has been sent.[38]

Rabbi Asher's ethical work based on an anthology of talmudic-midrashic sayings, *Perush Yud-Gimel Middot*, appears to be the earliest among the ethical works of the Gerona writers. It is possible, therefore, that it was he who began the literary enterprise in Gerona and that the others, like Nachmanides and Jacob ben Sheshet, followed him. If so, it is not farfetched to imagine that this new way was suggested by Rabbi Asher ben David on the basis of his mission as outlined by Rabbi Isaac the Blind's letter. It is as if Rabbi Asher were saying to his fellow mystics in Gerona: if our great teacher, Rabbi Isaac, forbade us from writing purely kabbalistic works, we should turn our efforts to another field—and why not ethics?

Rabbi Asher himself did not refrain from writing kabbalistic treatises, though they are brief and do not include profound discussions of kabbalistic problems. Nachmanides also wrote brief kabbalistic treatises and included some kabbalistic sections, written in a very esoteric manner which cannot be understood by the uninitiated, in his Commentary on the Pentateuch. Rabbi Jacob ben Sheshet did not hide his references to kabbalistic symbolism in his ethical and polemical works. This process, therefore, should not be viewed as a sharp, complete turnaway from writing Kabbalah and concentration on ethics. Rather, it seems to have been a gradual process, in which each of these kabbalists toned down the mystical terminology in his works and gradually increased his concentration on ethical teachings through the presentation of the ethics of the Talmud and Midrash.

One of the reasons for the emergence in Gerona in the first half of the thirteenth century of ethical literature based on the ancient sources may, therefore, have been this change in the manner of expression of these early mystics, brought about by Rabbi Isaac's letter and continued by the example set by Rabbi Isaac's emissary, Rabbi Asher ben David. On this background, it seems, we may suggest an answer to the question of the nature of Rabbi Jonah Gerondi's writing. It seems likely that Rabbi Jonah was indeed a kabbalist, a full member of the circle surrounding Nachmanides, and that the "Rabbi Jonah" in Rabbi Isaac's letter does indeed refer to him. The fact that his ethical works do not contain any kabbalistic symbols or ideas can be explained by the fact that all the other kabbalists in that circle gradually and in different ways refrained from expressing themselves fully concerning kabbalistic ideas. Rabbi Jonah was no different from them; he was simply more extreme in his adherence to Rabbi Isaac's demand that kabbalistic traditions be kept completely esoteric, and in the same way he followed in a more radical manner the new way—the composition of ethical works based on anthologies of ancient, traditional talmudic and midrashic sayings. The first four writers of this genre of ethics in Jewish culture were closely related members of the same small, esoteric school of mystics in Gerona.

VI

The fact that these four writers belonged to the Gerona school of kabbalists is not the only ideological element that ties them together. When we study the biography and world view of these authors it becomes apparent that there was another force binding them: opposition to the influence of Jewish philosophy, especially when the conflict between the supporters of Maimonidean philosophy and their traditionalist opponents reached its peak in 1232. The fierce outbreak of controversy at that time[39] was the result of the spread of the Hebrew translations of Maimonides' *Guide for the Perplexed* by Rabbi Judah Alharizi and by Rabbi Shmuel Ibn Tibbon.[40] The history of this conflict occupies a central place in Jewish history of the thirteenth century and has been studied by historians in great detail. Many questions are still unresolved, among them the connection between this conflict and the burning of the Talmud in Paris by the Church authorities in 1240; the scope of the ban declared against Maimonides' philosophy; and the problem of how and to what extent the rabbis of Germany and northern France participated in the controversy.[41]

Gershom Scholem has already pointed out the importance of the role of the kabbalists, especially those in Gerona, in the events of this controversy, and indeed, the more one studies this period the more apparent becomes the centrality of the activities of the kabbalists. The most obvious participant was Rabbi Jonah Gerondi, who was one of the first traditionalists to demand public action by the Jewish communities in northern Spain and in Provence against the spread of the philosophical teachings of Maimonides, and who was one of the first to suggest a public ban (*herem*) against the study of philosophy.[42] Throughout the years of the conflict Rabbi Jonah was a persistent opponent of any compromise and remained the leader of the anti-Maimonidean camp. A legend spread by Maimonides' supporters has it that his painful death was a punishment for his opposition to Maimonides, and that on his deathbed he repented and changed his mind.[43] There is nothing to support this legend among the known historical facts, and it seems, on the contrary, that Rabbi Jonah continued his struggle against Jewish philosophy until his death.

The major theological work of Rabbi Jacob ben Sheshet is not a work of ethics but a polemical, antiphilosophical treatise, *Meshiv Devarim Nechochim* ("A Refutation"). [44] As mentioned above, Rabbi Jacob wrote this work in order to refute the views concerning the creation and the whole theology expressed by Rabbi Shmuel Ibn Tibbon, the translator of *The Guide for the Perplexed.* The book contains an uncompromising critique, in a thorough, systematic manner, of the basic attitudes of Jewish philosophy. In this work Rabbi Jonah used many kabbalistic symbols, and there is no doubt that his adherence to the mystical views of the Gerona kabbalistic school served as a basis for his opposition to the new philosophy.

Although it was the mystical attitudes of Rabbi Jacob ben Sheshet that underlay his critique of philosophical cosmogony and cosmology, he expressed this opposition by the constant use of talmudic and midrashic sayings. His book is, to some extent, an impressive collection of ancient sections of the Talmud and Midrash on the subject, explained and analyzed by Rabbi Jacob according to his polemical purposes. His main argument against Rabbi Shmuel Ibn Tibbon is that the philosophy expressed by Rabbi Shmuel contradicts Jewish sacred tradition, and that the philosophical attempts to explain (often allegorically, always homiletically) the underlying harmony between Jewish tradition and philosophy are completely unconvincing. The position of Rabbi ben Sheshet is basically that of a traditionalist opposing a new system of thought. If he had not been a kabbalist, *Meshiv Devarim Nechochim* could still have been written, though the terminology and some emphases would have been different. There can be no doubt that Rabbi Jacob ben Sheshet belonged to the large group of rabbis in Provence and northern Spain who, under the leadership of Rabbi Jonah Gerondi and others, fought the spread of philosophical views in any way they could on the basis of the ancient traditions of Judaism.

When the controversy of 1232 began, Nachmanides was already in a position of leadership of the Jewish communities in Catalonia. The first document we have from him is an epistle directed mainly to the opponents of Maimonides.[45] In this epistle Nachmanides tried, as was his duty as a leader, to reduce tensions and to point out common ground for the two camps. He tried to argue that the philosophical, spiritual conception of God is not radically different from that of the traditionalists or even from that of the Ashkenazi Hasidim.[46] Nachmanides undoubtedly attempted in this epistle to maintain the position of an impartial mediator, trying to keep the conflict from spreading and deepening.

He could not maintain this position for long. In the heat of the controversy the supporters of Maimonides accused the family of Rabbi Jonah Gerondi of impurity, producing allegations of a forbidden marriage two generations before.[47] This accusation affected Nachmanides as well as his nephew, Rabbi Jonah, and in his later letters in this conflict Nachmanides takes the side of Rabbi Jonah and the other opponents of rationalistic philosophy.

While Nachmanides' public position in this controversy was shaped by his understanding of his role as a leader and by his family ties with Rabbi Jonah, he expressed his actual views concerning this conflict in his sermons. The most relevant ones to our subject are his treatments of the problems of the creation and of miracles in these sermons, for these two subjects were among the prominent ones dealt with by the opponents and the proponents of Maimonidean philosophy. Nachmanides' position is clear and unambiguous: his sermons attack fiercely the Aristotelian conceptions of an eternal, uncreated world, a world ruled by natural laws in which miracles are impossible.[48] He refutes the attempts made by some philosophers to harmonize biblical and talmudic descriptions of the creation and of historical miracles with the basic ideas of Aristotelian philosophy, and insists on the irreconcilable conflict between them. He has harsh words concerning Aristotle himself, who was, according to him, not only wrong but evil as well.

Nachmanides did not attack Maimonides directly, and he was

not alone in this forebearance. The prestige that Maimonides had acquired as the great author of the largest Jewish code of religious law, the *Mishneh Torah*, made many critics of the *Guide for the Perplexed* hesitate to attack him personally. It was much easier, and more customary, to criticize "Maimonides' disciples," who carelessly inferred from the teachings of Maimonides things that he himself would never have agreed to, or to attack non-Jewish philosophy, which served as a basis for the teachings of Maimonides. Though Nachmanides was careful not to confront squarely *The Guide for the Perplexed*, there can be no doubt concerning his complete opposition to the teachings of Jewish philosophy.

In his sermons Nachmanides seldom used kabbalistic symbolism. They could be read as purely traditionalistic refutations of the ideas of Aristotelian philosophy. Nachmanides, like Rabbi Jacob ben Sheshet, based his arguments on the clear meaning of biblical verses and talmudic sayings, proving that philosophical interpretation or harmonization of these sources with Aristotelian philosophy is impossible. In his case, too, while mysticism served as a hidden motive for his position, his arguments rely almost exclusively on traditional adherence to the ancient sources of Jewish belief.

Rabbi Asher ben David probably wrote his works before the outbreak of the great controversy of 1232 and subsequent years, and there is no direct reference to the issues of this conflict in these works. It is evident, however, from several statements in his kabbalistic and ethical treatises that the reasons for his opposition to the attitudes of the philosophers were similar to those of Rabbi Jonah, Rabbi Jacob ben Sheshet, and Nachmanides.[49]

VII

Thus four writers, in the small town of Gerona in Catalonia, shared common attitudes in three, seemingly unconnected, fields: (1) they were mystics, the receivers and developers of the kabbalistic ideas and symbols of the school of Rabbi Isaac the Blind, who accepted his ruling against the writing of kabbalistic works and the publicizing of their esoteric knowledge; (2) they were the first four writers of traditional, "rabbinic," ethical works in Hebrew in medieval Europe; and (3) they were active opponents of the spread of Aristotelian philosophy and the attempts to harmonize it with Jewish beliefs. It appears evident that for these writers the three different fields of literary and ideological activity—the Kabbalah, traditional ethics, and antiphilosophical polemics—constituted one whole. In these three ways they expressed their particular conception of what Judaism is and what it should be.

At the time these writers were active, Kabbalah was in its beginnings; very few traditions had already been developed and accepted. The first work in which kabbalistic symbolism can be found, the book *Bahir* ("The Book of Light"), was probably composed near the end of the twelfth century.[50] Its anonymous author undoubtedly used ancient traditions he received from the East—both mystical traditions from the school of the Hekhalot and Merkabah mysticism of the talmudic period, and unknown sources that included gnostic terminology and attitudes. To these he added a great deal of medieval material from the works of Rabbi Abraham bar Hijja and possibly even Rabbi Abraham Ibn Ezra.[51]

The *Bahir* was written in the form of a midrash, each section attributed to an ancient talmudic sage. It does not present a clear system; it sometimes even seems that the author tries intentionally to confuse and mislead the reader. Medieval kabbalists treated it as their main ancient source, believing that it originated in talmudic times and reflected esoteric traditions received by ancient Judaism and transmitted orally from generation to generation (this is why the Jewish mystics in medieval Europe called themselves "kabbalists," meaning "the recipients of an [esoteric] tradition").

The school of kabbalists in Provence at the end of the twelfth century and the beginning of the thirteenth probably had some independent mystical sources besides the teaching of the *Bahir*,[52] and Rabbi Isaac the Blind and others systematized this new Jewish mystical attitude and presented the Gerona circle with the beginning of a coherent set of symbols, which the Catalonia kabbalists continued to develop. But these two groups—in Provence and in Gerona—were extremely small, and had at that time almost no impact on the culture of the Jewish communities in which they lived. Some of these early kabbalists were teachers and leaders of their communities, like Nachmanides and the Rabad of Posquièrre, but they did not achieve this position of leadership because of their mystical expertise. They were regarded as leaders because of their leading position in the study and teaching of Jewish religious law, the halakhah, and their leadership qualities; there is no proof whatsoever that the fact that they were mystics played any role in their achieving such prominent positions in their communities.[53] The Kabbalah at that time was almost unknown, and not accepted as one of the legitimate aspects of Jewish religious culture. It is evident from Rabbi Isaac the Blind's letter that he preferred it this way and intended to do everything in his power to preserve Jewish mysticism as an esoteric aspect of religious expression known only by the few who were capable of accepting its teachings. As we have seen, Nachmanides and his circle in Gerona adhered to this preference of their great teacher.

Nachmanides and the other kabbalists of the Gerona circle had no ambition to teach and spread the Kabbalah to the masses. Their opposition to philosophy and to philosophical ethics was not based on their attempt to replace philosophy by Kabbalah (a process which began, indeed, in the sixteenth century and was accomplished by the seventeenth century).[54] The Kabbalah did not compete with Jewish philosophy, but it made the kabbalists stronger and more resolute opponents of philosophy.

It seems that the role of the emerging European Jewish mysticism in this context was first and foremost to strengthen the belief in the comprehensive nature and immeasurable depth of ancient Jewish tradition. A kabbalist in the thirteenth century was one who believed that beyond the literal and homiletical-midrashic meaning of the biblical verses there was another, greater truth, hidden and unknown except to a few mystics in every generation who transmitted these secrets in an oral tradition. The philosophers found Jewish tradition unable to answer contemporary problems, whether they were ideological, theological, or ethical-practical, and thus when they sought to present a new Judaism, based on logic and spirituality, they tried to harmonize Greek and Arabic philosophy with the talmudic sources. The kabbalists could not share this attitude; for them, what was insufficiently explained by the literal and homiletical interpretations of the Bible was profoundly elucidated through mystical symbolism.

In this way, the small circle of adherents to the Kabbalah in Gerona was unique in its time because of its deep confidence that the ancient Jewish sources contained relevant and complete answers to any problem that contemporary culture might present. They became the leaders of the opposition to philosophy mainly because of this deep, unshakable conviction.

But how to present the wide public with this deep conviction? Because of the prohibition by Rabbi Isaac the Blind, which they accepted in different degrees, they could not do this by teaching Kabbalah publicly or writing kabbalistic treatises. Instead, they hit upon the solution of composing traditional ethical works in which talmudic-midrashic ethics would be expounded, their richness and profound statements would be presented to the public, and thus the influence of philosophy would be negated. We may surmise that what added to the establishment of this literary form and ideological attitude was the fact that philosophical ethics was presented in such a radical way that it was practically cut off from any inherent ideological connection with ancient Jewish sources. The need for the establishment of a connection between everyday behavior and ancient tradition was more apparent because of the way that Jewish philosophical ethics was presented by its authors.

It would be wrong to conclude that the Kabbalah was the source of the emergence of traditional, antiphilosophical Jewish ethics in the Middle Ages. The same conclusions could be reached, and were reached, independently of the Kabbalah. The proof is the ethical work, *Ma'alot ha-midot*, written in Italy by Rabbi Yehiel ben Yekutiel of Rome in the thirteenth century,[55] an anthology of talmudic and midrashic ethics, which offered an alternative to the influence of philosophical ethics. We have no evidence that Rabbi Yehiel was a kabbalist, and the book does not contain any hint that the author was aware of mystical attitudes. Apparently Rabbi Yehiel independently (though, chronologically, somewhat later) reached the same conclusions as the Gerona circle of kabbalists, without being assisted by the Kabbalah. But this cannot change the fact that the first school of traditional ethics, the four writers discussed above, derived its strength from its adherence to the mytical traditions of the *Bahir* and of Rabbi Isaac the Blind.

This fact, rooted in immediate, specific circumstances of the early thirteenth century, conveys an important historical aspect of Jewish ethical literature. Following the teachings of Rabbi Isaac in Provence, the early kabbalists in Gerona developed a radical, innovative system of ideas within Judaism: the concept of the ten *sefirot*, the divine emanations, and the revolutionary reinterpretation of the Bible and the talmudic legends based on these symbols. At the same time, these same mystics introduced into Jewish culture the most conservative system of ethics, claiming, in fact, that nothing should be added to the old, traditional, talmudic sources. This paradoxical fusion of radical innovation and conservative traditionalism is, as we shall see below, an inherent characteristic of Jewish ethical literature. In the period described in this chapter Jewish ethics survived the revolution of the introduction of Jewish philosophy, the radical spiritualization represented by Bahya Ibn Paquda, and the appearance of the kabbalistic mystical system—and it still preserved its strong adherence to the early talmudic sources.

At the same time, or even a decade or two earlier, in another part of Europe, another school of Jewish esoteric writers and mystics presented a system of traditional Jewish ethics. This was the Ashkenazi Hasidic movement, the Jewish pietists of medieval

Germany. We should study their version of the fusion of mysticism and traditional ethics before presenting final conclusions concerning the relationship between mysticism and ethics in the history of Jewish culture in medieval Europe.

3

MYSTICISM AND ETHICS
IN THE ASHKENAZI HASIDIC
MOVEMENT

DURING THE LAST decades of the twelfth century and the first decades of the thirteenth there appeared in the Jewish communities in western Germany, mainly in the Rhineland, a whole literature of esoteric theological character. The two greatest authors of this literature were Rabbi Judah ben Shmuel ben Kalonymus, known as Rabbi Judah the Pious, and his disciple, Rabbi Eleazar ben Judah ben Kalonymus, known as Rabbi Eleazar of Worms.[1] These two writers were the prominent leaders of a distinct movement within Ashkenazi Jewry, the Ashkenazi Hasidic movement, the pietistic movement of German Jewry in the Middle Ages.[2] In addition to their voluminous theological works these two writers created an important ethical literature which had a profound influence on all subsequent Jewish works in the field of ethics, especially from the sixteenth century to the present. In this chapter we shall examine the relationship between mystical theology and pietistic ethics in the works of these two writers and in the Ashkenazi Hasidic movement as a whole.

Like the kabbalists in southern France and northern Spain, the Ashkenazi Hasidim insisted that their esoteric doctrines were not their own discovery but had been received in a long chain of tradition from the sages of ancient Judaism.[3] We have several versions of a description of the way these secrets were transmitted, in a document that Rabbi Eleazar of Worms included in his great Commentary on the prayers. According to this description,[4] German pietists from the Kalonymus family brought the tradition with them when they emigrated from southern Italy to Mainz in the ninth century, and from that time it was transmitted from father to son and from a rabbi to his disciple, until it reached Rabbi Judah the Pious and his disciples.[5] According to Rabbi Eleazar, the esoteric tradition reached the Kalonymus family in Italy in the eighth century, when a scholar and magician from Babylonia, Rabbi Aharon ben Shmuel of Baghdad, came to Italy and taught the rabbis there, who were already interested in the Hekhalot and Merkabah mysticism, the mystical meaning of the prayers and other esoteric traditions.[6]

In various places in their works the Ashkenazi Hasidim repeatedly claimed that their teachings were derived from ancient sources and from continuous chains of oral tradition concerning the interpretation of mystical texts like the *Sefer Yezirah* ("The Book of Creation" from the talmudic period) and the Hekhalot texts. In cosmological matters they relied, among others, on the great scholar and physician of tenth-century Italy, Rabbi Shabbatai Donolo.

One of the schools of the Ashkenazi mystics created a whole myth to explain the source of their tradition. They claimed that they had in their possession an ancient text, a *barayta*, written by Joseph ben Uziel, who was described as the grandson of Ben Sira (Ecclesiasticus), and the great-grandson of the prophet Jeremiah.[7] According to them, these secrets had been revealed by Jeremiah in Babylonia and then transmitted to Ben Sira, to his son Uzziel, to his son Joseph, and Joseph's writings reached the medieval mystics in a long chain of tradition and interpretation. Another legend connects the mystical tradition with a mysterious Joseph Maon, who was supposed to have been exiled from Jerusalem to Rome by the emperor Titus when the temple in Jerusalem was destroyed, and who became the source of their knowledge.

The main group of Ashkenazi Hasidim, those of the school of

Rabbi Judah the Pious and Rabbi Eleazar of Worms, did not use such crude pseudoepigraphy to add sanctity to their traditions. Nevertheless, they not only insisted, but seemed sincerely to believe, that what they were writing was not new. All they were doing was writing down and publishing to a small circle of disciples traditions that had existed within Judaism for many centuries. The reason for this insistence was undoubtedly the rejection of any logical or analytical way of reaching the truth. All truth must be ancient, and if it is ancient it must have been transmitted from the sages of the East to the mystics of the West. Antiquity and traditionalism were the proof of the veracity of the content of their theological speculations. In this conviction they resemble very closely the attitude of the early kabbalists in southern Europe, though there is one important difference: the kabbalists not only insisted on the traditional character of their knowledge; they also claimed to have had mystical revelations to confirm this, such as the appearance of the prophet Elijah in the schools of the early kabbalists in Provence in the twelfth century.[8] In Germany, although we do find reliance on such revelations, these are mostly in the realm of halakhah, when legal problems are solved by direct communication from heaven. We do not find such claims concerning mystical, cosmological, or theological secrets, since in these fields the claim that the contents of these traditions were transmitted orally from generation to generation apparently sufficed to give them religious authenticity.

The vast difference between Ashkenazi Hasidic ethics and its theological works is one of the central problems concerning the history of the beginnings of Hebrew ethical literature in the Middle Ages: the Ashkenazi Hasidim did not describe any ancient, traditional source which reached them and revealed their original ethical teachings. They present and discuss the requirements of everyday life in the realms of social ethics, as well as concerning the relationship between man and God, without giving any specific source of authority to prove the authenticity of their demands. They very often rely on biblical verses or talmudic sayings for support for their ideas, but the structure as a whole is presented without any explanation of why the reader should accept their views rather than somebody else's.

This basic difference in attitude toward ethics, as opposed to theology, is one of the reasons why the problem of the relationship between ethics and theology in the structure of the world view of the Ashkenazi Hasidim should be studied in detail. I shall, therefore, present first a brief outline of their mysticism and theology, and then the main points of their ethical teachings, and finally, attempt a synthesis of the two, pointing out the interrelationship between ethics and esoteric, mystical theology in Jewish communities of medieval Germany.

II

Ashkenazi Hasidic esoteric theology dealt with all the central problems of a religious world view: the problems of the nature of the creation, of miracles, of cosmology and divine providence, anthropology and psychology, angelology and demonology, and many other subjects.[9] The discussion of these problems is not systematic; the Ashkenazi Hasidim were not exposed to the influence of Greek philosophy either through the Arabic authors who utilized it or through Christian theologians who wrote mostly in Latin, with which they were not familiar.[10] Their deep hatred of the Christian church and the culture that surrounded it created an unbridgeable gulf between the teachers of Ashkenazi Hasidim and the systematic theology of their time in central Europe. This hatred was the result of the persecution of the Jews of Germany and northern France during the period of the Crusades, a period in which thousands of Jews died at the hands of the crusaders or by their own hands rather than convert to Christianity. The impact of these persecutions, which recurred several times from 1096 to the beginning of the thirteenth century, on their theology and ethics was enormous, and one of the consequences was that they wrote their works in traditional Jewish literary forms without being influenced by the development around them of systematic theology in Arabic and in Latin.

Among the various subjects studied by the Ashkenazi Hasidim in their esoteric theology, the most central were those in which the problem of the direct relationship between man and God was most clearly manifest, namely, divine revelation, prayer, and divine providence. The basic theological questions are: What did the prophets see in their visions? To whom does one pray? What is the relationship between man's deeds and the way God provides for the world? We may say that the subject of divine revelation in its widest meaning is central to the theological discussions of the Ashkenazi Hasidim. At the same time it becomes obvious that this kind of theology is most open to the inclusion of mystical elements, for mysticism also deals with the subject of the meeting between man and God. And indeed, the mystical element in Ashkenazi Hasidic speculations is related to their conclusions concerning the nature of divine revelation.

Like the kabbalists in southern Europe, the Ashkenazi Hasidim developed a system of powers emanating from God to explain various aspects of the revelation of God to the world and to man. They could not accept the view of Rav Saadia Gaon[11] that what the prophets saw was nothing but a created angel, a power that God brought forth specifically for the purpose of showing the prophets a sign of the divine nature of the message revealed in the prophecy. The role of prophecy in the Ashkenazi Hasidic system was too exalted and central to be entrusted to a created, secondary power.[12] Instead, they described in great detail the divine power, emanating from God and constituting an integral part of Him, retaining its completely divine nature, which was revealed to the prophets— the divine glory, the *kavod*, also called the *shekhinah*. According to them, this power is connected to God in one "face," which is turned upward toward God, while its other "face" is turned toward the created world. When Moses saw God, as described in the thirty-third chapter of Exodus, God explained to him that His

cf
Levinas
(1)

"upper face," where the *kavod* is connected with God Himself, can never be seen, but the "face" that is turned toward the created beings can be revealed, and indeed, this is the source of all prophecy.[13] This is also what all the righteous will behold in heaven, after their death. They will be sitting around the enormous throne of glory, over which the divine glory is revealed, and the supreme bliss that these righteous will enjoy is the divine light emanating from the divine glory.[14]

The theory of the divine glory as an emanated divine power assisted the Ashkenazi Hasidim when they tried to explain the nature of prayer.[15] The teachings of Rav Saadia Gaon, and theological ideas that they received from other sources, made the Hasidim distinguish between the Godhead, which is omnipresent and omniscient, and the divine power that sustains and guides the created world. The Godhead cannot change in any way, and therefore cannot be the divine power that the religious person addresses when he prays. Prayer in the traditional manner implies that God listens to the requests of the religious person as if these were new information, and then makes the decision whether to comply with his wishes or not. It means that God changes when he receives the requests and again when he fulfills them or does not fulfill them. The Ashkenazi Hasidim, even though they were not familiar with logical, systematic theological analysis, perceived that the Godhead cannot be the recipient of prayers because he is omniscient and no change can apply to Him. Again, the divine glory was the answer: it is to this lower divine power that prayers are addressed.

The Ashkenazi Hasidim developed a unique theology concerning the relationship between the divine glory and the supreme Godhead (which they usually call, paradoxically, "The Creator"). According to them, the Godhead cannot be revealed in any way, is not subject to change, and is transcendental; it is described in a manner not greatly different from the prime cause of the Aristotelian philosophers, as Nachmanides noted in his epistle of 1232.[16] At the same time, the Godhead is completely immanent, present within everything and around everything in the same constant way, because nothing, not even dirt, evil, or sin can stop Him or create a boundary that He cannot penetrate. [17] But the equal way in which He is immanent within everything makes this immanence meaningless concerning the nature of the created things within which He is present. Since He is always the same, everywhere and at every time, His presence does not change the character of these beings, and it does not have any effect on their behavior and development, because He cannot react to any change that occurs in the world within which He is present. The Godhead is the source of all existence, but He does not affect the ways in which this existence is changing.

There is, however, another kind of immanence, that of the divine glory. The glory is not present everywhere; it is where it chooses to be, where it can be and should be. It is absent from any place that is dirty or evil. It can and does remove itself from any place where sin is committed. It is present in synagogues and where the righteous congregate. It is the worker of miracles and the power revealed to the prophets. It directs history, rewards the just, and punishes the wicked. This is a kind of selective immanence, a divine presence that is directly responsible for the guidance and direction of the world.

From these original conceptions the Ashkenazi Hasidim developed a view of nature and the world directly opposite to that of the philosophers and, indeed, to that of most other theologians, Jewish and non-Jewish alike. The laws that govern nature are constant and eternal ones. These laws have very few exceptions, which we designate as miracles. The miracles are the result of the direct intervention of the divine glory in the natural sphere in order to carry out some benevolent and just divine decision. This means that the unchanged law does not reflect divine benevolence; only the miraculous exception does. It is as if the constant laws are governed by the Godhead and are, therefore, unchanging and do not care for the specific needs of the righteous, whether an individual or a people. God's care for his servants is revealed only when these laws are broken by the benevolent intervention of the divine glory. Therefore, the general way in which the world is governed does not reflect divine goodness; this goodness becomes apparent only when the laws are suspended and a miracle occurs.

According to this system, Rabbi Judah the Pious explained the way in which man can come to know divine goodness.[18] Unlike the philosophers, who usually preached the examination of the wonderful structure of the creation in order to understand God, Rabbi Judah stated that anyone who wishes to recognize God's goodness should look for the exceptional, the miraculous. Long sections in his esoteric works are dedicated to the analysis of biblical stories of the miracles in order to learn from them the nature of God's benevolence. For him, a "miracle" was not only an event that happened just once; he included in this category some phenomena that we usually regard as natural law rather than miracle.

For instance, Rabbi Judah raised the question: how is it possible that God (and the context clearly proves that he means the divine glory) can hear at the same time the prayers of people from all parts of the world, listen to them, and answer them? His answer is: God gave us a sign that he could do this, and indeed does this, in a miracle found among us. A man cannot hear many things at once, as he cannot taste or touch many things at the same time. So it seems that the general law governing human senses is that they react to phenomena one after the other, in a sequence, and not at the same time. But God gave our eyes the power to see many things, many colors, in one glance. This is miraculous; it is a wonderful gift given to man by God so that he will believe that God himself can hear as well as see many things at once, including the prayers of thousands of people in different parts of the world. God's benevolence cannot be perceived by the scientific analysis of the general laws; only when studying the exceptional, the unusual, can one begin to understand the nature of the goodness of God. Science, therefore, does not reveal a way toward God; only by the identification of nonscientific phenomena can one glean an understanding of the nature of the divine.

The works of the Ashkenazi Hasidim, and especially those of

Rabbi Judah the Pious, are a treasure house of descriptions of the demonic powers, witches, spirits of the dead, vampires and werewolves, and all other supernatural phenomena. [19] The unusual interest in this field, unparalleled in its scope in Hebrew medieval literature and unusual in European literature of the time, is the direct result of Rabbi Judah's attitude toward miracles. The investigation of the unusual and the miraculous is, according to his theology, the way to understand God's goodness; therefore it is the first duty of the theologian to collect such phenomena and examine them. Witchcraft and demonology are naturally the realms in which the extraordinary and the supernatural most often occur; therefore, here God's ways are to be studied. The Ashkenazi Hasidim did not develop a dualistic attitude, viewing demons and witches as representatives of an evil principle. These were for them usual worldly phenomena; supernatural, but part of the order of things in a world governed by only one principle, one God. There is no concept of the devil or Satan as the ruler of the demonic realm. Therefore, they did not hesitate to study some of the most extreme, even cruel, demonic phenomena in order to glean from them a theological insight into the goodness of God, which cannot be derived from the natural laws that govern all existence.

One example may demonstrate this attitude. The Ashkenazi Hasidim describe in detail, in a dozen or more places in their theological works, a practice of divination that was probably brought to Europe from the East through the influence of the Arabs, and is still known and practiced in the Middle East and elsewhere. This was the practice of finding out a hidden fact— usually where a lost ring can be found, or who stole a certain object—by having a child gaze into a bright surface covered with oil. The child perceives in the oil the image of a demon, who, when forced to do so by the formulas spoken by the sorcerer, reveals in the oil a picture of the stolen or lost object and where it is hidden or who stole it. The child tells the sorcerer what he sees, for the people around the child see nothing. [20] A modern skeptic would explain this as a result of psychological suggestion, and it may be for this reason that the practitioners of this procedure always insisted that it should be carried out by a very young child.

Rabbi Judah the Pious and Rabbi Eleazar of Worms were fascinated by this practice, and it is not difficult to understand why. They bring up the subject whenever they are dealing with the appearance of the divine glory to the prophets, as described in the Bible. Why is it that the prophet saw whatever he saw, that is, an image of the divine glory, while people around him did not? The answer is that this is one of the aspects of the miracle of revelation which negates natural laws. But in order that people will believe that such wonderful occurrences as the divine revelation are possible, God gave common sorcerers the ability to perform something that slightly resembles the divine process. When the child sees in the oil things that are true (as proven by the subsequent finding of the lost or stolen object), but no one else who looks into the same bright surface can see anything, God has demonstrated His power to be revealed to the prophet, and to no one else.

The Ashkenazi Hasidim treated such phenomena, both of past miracles and of contemporary supernatural occurrences, as the realm in which God's goodness, which is not manifest in the general laws of nature, can be perceived. This is in direct opposition to the way in which most philosophers treated nature. For them, the general laws were the revelation of God's goodness, while the miracles presented a most difficult theological problem: they were embarrassing testimonies to the imperfection of the creation, which has to be "corrected" from time to time by miraculous exceptions to the laws. The Ashkenazi Hasidim took the opposite view: it is the miracles which testify to the goodness of God, whereas the general laws are neutral; this idea is one of the most relevant theological concepts for the formulation of the Ashkenazi Hasidic ethical system.

III

Can Ashkenazi Hasidic esoteric theology be described as mystical? Gershom Scholem included a chapter on this movement in his *Major Trends in Jewish Mysticism*, but did not clearly designate the pietists as mystics.[21] Many chapters of their books of theological speculations have nothing to do with mysticism. A full answer to this question would require a more extensive discussion of the meaning of mysticism than is possible here. But there are several elements in their conception of religious life that denote a tendency toward what is usually regarded as a mystical attitude.

This is evident in the fact that the Ashkenazi Hasidim dedicated most of their efforts to the collection, presentation, and elucidation of the ancient Hebrew mystical sources, the Hekhalot and Merkabah literature.[22] Most of the texts of the mystical schools which are known today are found in manuscript collections prepared by the Ashkenazi Hasidim. Many of their works are commentaries and anthologies of this ancient mystical material. They wrote books on the meaning of the Holy Name of God, presented lists of angels and supreme powers, and dwelt especially on the hidden powers within the Hebrew letters, following the tradition of the ancient *Sefer Yezirah*. There can be no doubt that they were keenly interested in the mystical visions of the divine world as presented in the mysticism of the talmudic period.

Was their study of Hekhalot mysticism completely speculative? Did they merely copy, interpret, and re-present the mysticism of the ancients, or did they also try to follow it, to ascend to the divine world like the talmudic sages? We do not have any clear proof that they did so, though scattered remarks in their works denote that they may have. They insisted on a purification ceremony before the secret of the Holy Name could be taught by a master to a disciple, and in one case at least we know that they gave a practical meaning to the ancient texts they studied: they dealt with the creation of a *golem*, a homunculus, following certain interpretations of the *Sefer Yezira*.[23] They may have done so also concerning the practice of the "descent to the divine chariot," the chief mystical procedure described in Hekhalot mysticism.

Probably the closest the Ashkenazi Hasidim came to mystical

practice was in connection with the meaning of the daily prayers. The Ashkenazi Hasidim insisted on the acceptance of every word and every letter of the Jewish prayers without the slightest change, even though they recognized, as is common in Jewish tradition, that the prayers had been composed by the sages of the Second Commonwealth and later.[24] The Ashkenazi Hasidim, however, discovered a secret layer of meaning in the prayers, a numerical harmony that existed in the number of words, letters, names, and the numerical value of groups of letters (*gematria*) throughout sacred literature. Nothing in the prayers was accidental; every letter was part of a numerical harmony, which is reflected in the Bible and indeed throughout the world. The prayers are not merely words conveying a meaning; this is only their superficial, external appearance. They include within their intricate numerical structure a divine harmony, which is the reflection of the divine, and its counterparts can be found in all other parts of God's words and deeds. Rabbi Judah the Pious's lost magnum opus, of which only a collection of quotations is extant, was a commentary on the prayers, written in several large volumes and completely dedicated to the demonstration of this numerical harmony. It was probably the first commentary on the prayers to be written, though immediately afterward other commentaries followed, both by Ashkenazi Hasidim, such as Rabbi Eleazar of Worms, and by early kabbalists.

It is not clear whether the demonstration of the numerical harmony in prayers was intended by Rabbi Judah the Pious and his followers to be only theoretical, or whether it had consequences concerning the religious practice of praying. Was it enough for the pietist to know that such a harmony existed and understand it, or should this play a part in the religious experience of facing God in the synagogue and uttering those words? It is very difficult to prove that the Ashkenazi Hasidim insisted on the practical side of this system, but it undoubtedly was an integral part of their conception of religious achievement. In this we may perceive a definite leaning toward a mystical view of prayers and of religious ritual as a whole.

These and other details are very important for an analysis of mystical character of the Ashkenazi Hasidic movement and its esoteric doctrines. But no less important is the general attitude found in their works, that of the negation of the divine, benevolent character of the laws by which nature, society, and even man are governed, and the insistence on the miraculous character of divine revelation, which is the only means by which divine goodness is introduced into the world. Though God is everywhere and within everything, divine goodness is not. The pietist has to seek and discover the scattered, hidden manifestations of the divine goodness, and find them in the most improbable places. The aim of religious life and ethics is to point a way out of the nondivine existence within natural laws and find the path toward the hidden, selective goodness which does not characterize creation. This quest can indeed be described as mystical.

How did the Ashkenazi Hasidim translate their theology and mystical attitudes into ethical values and directions for an ethical way of life? This endeavor was central to their system, and they dedicated a large part of their activity to teaching ethics in a popular form, while they kept their theological doctrines hidden and esoteric. It is for this reason that their theology had only little impact on subsequent developments in Jewish thought, while their ethics became a dominant system, shaping Jewish ethics for centuries to come.

IV

Jewish ethical systems in the Middle Ages were faced with a basic paradox, which shaped their values and their practical demands: the contrast between what Judaism was and what was regarded as the nature of religion in the Middle Ages; between what was and what should have been. The process of the adaptation of Judaism to the religious norms of the medieval period is the process of the spiritualization of Judaism, which was carried out within ethical thought and ethical literature.

When Jewish thinkers became aware of the ideological and religious atmosphere around them, about the tenth century, the basic conceptions of Greek philosophy as translated into monotheistic thought were already shaping medieval religious thought. The dualistic contradiction between matter and spirit, body and soul, derived from Platonic and neo-Platonic as well as Aristotelian philosophies, was already central to both Christian and Moslem thought. Religion was the expression of the spiritual side of man, which was in constant conflict with his material, physical side. God was conceived as the supreme spiritual power, and everything material was therefore nondivine. Ethics and religious ritual were the servants of the soul in its attempt to overcome the obstacles presented by the material world and the human body and to approach in spirit the spiritual God.

All Jewish thinkers of the Middle Ages not only recognized this basic attitude, but adopted it as their own. The dualism of spirit versus matter, soul against the body, became central to Jewish religious and ethical thought as it was to the other monotheistic religions.

The adoption of the spiritual conception of religion by Judaism was much more difficult than for Christianity, and to some extent even for Islam, because of the large body of religious laws and ethics which Judaism inherited from ancient times, and which no Jew— as long as he remained within the framework of Judaism—wished to discard or minimize in importance. The hundreds of Jewish religious laws (*mitzvot*) and ethical directions were all concentrated around physical behavior: when and how to wash one's hands, what to eat and what not to, what to do on the Sabbath and what was forbidden, how to conduct the sexual aspect of life, detailed laws concerning social behavior, and all the other subjects that constitute the legal and the ethical parts of the Bible and the Talmud. Ancient Judaism, unaware of the concept of dualistic conflict between body and soul, insisted on a physical expression of every religious and ethical practice. Things done only in the heart or mind were not regarded as part of the actual performance of what

God demanded from man. Everything had to find its expression through the actual physical expression of a feeling or an idea. There was even argument over whether it was religiously meaningful if one coupled thought and intention to a deed or not, and the tendency was to insist on the deed and all but disregard the intention. Thus Judaism seemed, even to its own most dedicated practitioners, to be extremely physical and remote from the spiritual ideal. If we take into account that the existence of Judaism in the Middle Ages was in a context of constant competition with the other monotheistic religions, which sought to convince Jews to convert, we may realize how crucial was this problem, for it seemed to present Judaism as an inferior, nonspiritual set of religious and ethical demands when compared to the other religions.

It was the duty of Jewish medieval thinkers, and first and foremost among them that of the writers of ethical works, to prove that what was apparent was not real, and that Judaism was indeed a spiritual religion, which put primary emphasis on spiritual ethics and the spiritual meaning of ritual, like, and even more than, Christianity and Islam. The discovery of the spiritual aspect of Judaism and its dominance over the physical aspect is the main subject of Jewish ethical literature in the Middle Ages. This is the reason why this literature deals much more with the question of why a man should do something than with the classical ethical question of what should be done. The "what" is clearly defined by the biblical and talmudic halakhic and ethical demands. The problem was to explain why, and by answering to demonstrate the spiritual character of Jewish faith and practice.

Jewish ethical literature developed four distinct answers to this problem, four systems which correspond to the major Jewish spiritual movements of the Middle Ages. The first was that of the Jewish philosophers; the second, that of the Ashkenazi Hasidim; the third, that of the "rabbinic" writers; and the fourth, the mystical answer of the kabbalists. The Ashkenazi Hasidic solution will be discussed below; that of the kabbalists in the next chapter. A brief outline of the "rabbinic" and philosophical solution was

presented in the previous chapter. The system of Rabbi Bahya Ibn
Paquda, for instance, is a good example of the way the Jewish
philosophers chose to confront this problem. Their usual attitude
was to add another dimension, a superstructure of spiritual demands, beyond the physical deeds required by Jewish law.

This could be achieved by either designing a separate set of
spiritual requirements, as Bahya did in his "duties of the heart," or
by discovering an allegorical layer of meaning inside the practical
demands themselves, which thus became representatives of spiritual values rather than self-justifying physical deeds. Later generations of Jews, especially from the sixteenth century onward, tended
to feel that the philosophical solution to the problem of spiritualization negatively affected the authority of religious law, and
put the emphasis elsewhere. If the deed was not important in itself
but was representative of a spiritual value, why could not that value
be represented by another, more "modern" or "logical" deed? The
Ashkenazi Hasidim, however, do not seem to have been acquainted
with the philosophical answers, and it is most probable that they
developed their system in isolation, reflecting their own needs and
their specific historical circumstances.

The Ashkenazi Hasidic solution to the problem of spiritualization was the direct result of their theological conceptions. Divine
goodness was not to be found in the laws of nature. In the same way,
it was not to be found in the structure of man's body or psyche. God
did not create man as an ideal creature, who, if he followed his
human nature, would achieve religious purity. Human nature and
human desires exist in contradiction to the demands of God, and in
order to approach God, man has to overcome his humanity.

In order to enable man to achieve this, God supplied him with
the necessary means: religious and ethical laws, the *mitzvot* and the
ethical values he has to follow in his deeds. These commandments
are not intended to enable man to reach pleasurable perfection, as
Rav Saadia, for instance, suggested, if they were performed in the
necessary harmony. They have, according to the Ashkenazi
Hasidim, one purpose only: to test the human spirit when it has to

choose between the spiritual and the material, between body and soul.

When the teachers of Ashkenazi Hasidic ethics wished to encourage the reader to adhere strictly to their doctrines, they repeatedly used one central argument: imagine that you are in a situation of *kidush ha-shem*, that is, you are presented with the choice between death and conversion to Christianity by the crusaders who surround you, as so often happened in the Jewish communities in Germany at that time. There is no doubt, they say, that you will choose death rather than adopt another religion (as thousands of Jews really did). If one is ready to give God the supreme sacrifice, why hesitate concerning the relatively minor daily practice under discussion? If one is ready to submit to God one's whole life, body and soul, even to torture and death, can one not make the necessary effort to follow this or that ritualistic or ethical demand?

This argument is repeated so often, with such deep conviction of its power of persuasion, that we have every right to infer that in it the Ashkenazi Hasidim expressed their basic attitude toward law and ethics. While *kidush ha-shem* opened before the pietist the gates of heaven, it certainly was not intended by God to support and fulfill man's humanity. Quite to the contrary, the divine demand was intended to enable man to sacrifice his humanity for the sake of God, to prove to himself and demonstrate to others his dedication to the spirit over matter and body.

What is true about the supreme demand, *kidush ha-shem*, is also true about the most minute daily practices of ritual and ethical behavior. One should view them as small, partial examples of *kidush ha-shem*. Like it, they are not demanded by God because they are beneficial to human life or enjoyable in any way. They were selected by God because he saw in them examples of the overcoming of the body by the soul. The Jew who refrains from certain foods, not because they are harmful or unesthetic, but even though they are good, sacrifices their enjoyment for the sake of God. He has not performed a physical deed but a spiritual one; he has dedicated a part of his human desires to God by refraining from the enjoyment that the food offered. If this is so, the commandments are to be measured by the spiritual force necessary for their performance, and not by the nature of the deed itself.

A good example of this attitude is offered by Rabbi Judah the Pious.[25] One of the most important ethical demands of the time was the release of Jews taken into captivity by gentiles and offered for sale as slaves. It was regarded as a supreme duty of every person to do his best to collect the ransom necessary to free the captive Jew. Now, if a ship carrying a Jewish captive reaches a town, and a poor Jew sets out to collect the money to save him, traveling from place to place and gathering, with much difficulty, the required sum; but finds when he returns that the prisoner has already been set free by a rich Jew who paid the ransom without much difficulty, who has earned more in terms of religious and ethical values: the rich Jew who actually performed the ethical deed, or the poor Jew who demonstrated more strongly his spiritual adherence to this value?

If we follow the basic, spiritualistic attitude of the Ashkenazi Hasidim, the conclusion is inevitable, and indeed Rabbi Judah the Pious formulated it: the one who made the greater effort, who suffered more and sacrificed more for the purpose of achieving ethical perfection, is the more righteous one. What counts is not the deed, but the effort and the suffering. The Ashkenazi Hasidim used the old Aramaic slogan, *"lefum za'ara agra,"* meaning, "The reward is according to the suffering."

It should be emphasized that this system does not open even the slightest possibility for the neglect of the deed itself and concentration on the spiritual side at the expense of the actual performance of the ethical deed. When the "suffering" is defined as the actual efforts made in order to perform the commandment, if one hesitates or minimizes the importance of the physical deed, there is no direction and no measuring rod for one's spiritual efforts. One cannot sit at home and "strive" spiritually to free the Jewish captive; it is the physical effort that counts, even when the act of liberating the captive was done by somebody else. The various rituals and ethical demands are tests presented by God to the righteous; there can be no substitute for striving to fulfill them. No one can devise another, "better," set of tasks, because the very attempt to substitute something else is first and foremost an evasion of the test put forward by God before man, and is viewed as a trick by the physical, evil element inside man to neglect divine demands. In this way the Ashkenazi Hasidic system is most radical in, at the same time, emphasizing the spiritual meaning of religious and ethical life, and preserving complete orthodoxy concerning the full adherence to the legal and ethical norms as set by ancient Judaism. The commandments are, on the one hand, meaningless, because if they are performed easily and with enjoyment they do not contribute to man's religious achievement; but, on the other hand, they and they alone are the source of such achievement by being the goals set before man by God in order to test his ability to sacrifice himself for God.

In a treatise by Rabbi Eleazar of Worms, dedicated to the study of human psychology, this conception is generalized in a surprising theological manner.[26] According to Rabbi Eleazar (and the same idea is found also in Rabbi Judah the Pious's work), when God wanted to create the world, he failed a few times before creating the present one. He first tried to devise a world in which man would have in him nothing but evil desires, and still would be required to become righteous. These attempts failed, because not even two righteous persons existed in those worlds, and God had to destroy them. Only then did God choose a compromise, creating man not only with evil inclinations but also with some good ones to assist him to achieve righteousness. In this world some righteous persons did exist, and therefore the world has not been destroyed.

According to this thesis, which is based on a homiletical exegesis of a few verses from the Book of Job, the ideal world is the perfectly evil one! If God could have had his way completely, nothing good would have been found in the world. This is the ideal state, because then, if someone attains the status of a righteous person, he has really achieved it without any outside assistance.

His righteousness would then be perfect and complete, achieved against maximum odds and therefore requiring maximum efforts. We can put it in another way: perfect righteousness means the achievement of the impossible. It is the task of God to put a maximum of obstacles in front of man (and within him), so that he can overcome them and reach the status of the righteous. If God makes the effort easier, He immediately detracts from the maximum possible achievement, thus harming man and preventing him from reaching the heights he is capable of.

What, according to this, is the meaning of the Torah and the Talmud and all the body of religious and ethical requirements of Judaism? Are they "good" or "bad"? They are the obstacle course set by God in order to test man. They should, by their purpose, be as difficult, unenjoyable, and harsh as humanly possible—or even more than that. When the Ashkenazi Hasidim write about the righteous, they do not mean every pietist or even most of them. They claim that the existence of two righteous persons throughout history is enough to assure the existence of the world. The example given by them for such a righteous person is David, probably because the biblical narrative does not leave any doubt concerning the existence of great evil drives within him. The commandments are therefore undoubtedly "bad" for man's humanity, for his wish to enjoy his life in the world, but they are beneficial in the long run because they enable him to try to achieve righteousness by overcoming the difficulties inherent in the performance of the ritualistic and ethical demands and thus be a candidate for everlasting bliss after death.

This attitude is also apparent in the Ashkenazi Hasidic conceptions concerning repentance, which occupy a central place in their ethical works.[27] In order to atone, a person has first to be punished for his transgressions. This punishment means the acceptance, in a voluntary way, of suffering and even self-torture. This is necessary in order to serve as a balance for the pleasure the transgressor derived from the performance of the sin. The underlying belief is that sin must cause pleasure, as righteousness must cause pain. One cannot return to the path of the righteous unless one has rid himself of the pleasure he had derived from the commitment of the sin by taking upon himself "extra" pain and suffering. This self-torture usually takes the form of long fasts, but sometimes more picturesque forms, like immersion in icy water in the winter or lying naked on an anthill in the summer. It should, however, be emphasized that the Ashkenazi Hasidim clearly limited these forms of self-torture only to the sinner who wished to repent; they did not recommend them to the righteous who wanted to achieve perfection; for him it is as if the "tortures" or the suffering prescribed by the Torah are enough. He does not have to seek any more, for God has already devised the perfect proportion for this purpose in His legal and ethical demands.

This is the paradoxical nature of the Ashkenazi Hasidic ethics. The good is to be achieved through the bad; the divine demands seem to be harsh and contradict human nature because they are intended to lead the believer to righteousness, which cannot be attained unless one fully accepts the measure of suffering and hardships that God has allotted him in His code of law and system of ethics.

V

When the Ashkenazi Hasidim presented their system of repentance, they set out two conflicting courses for the behavior of the penitent after he has accepted the punishment and suffered as he should for the pleasure he had derived from his sin. One way is to take upon himself extremely strict prohibitions which will make certain that he shall never repeat his transgression;[28] if he sinned with a woman, he should decide not even to see a woman or her clothes, and should take many other steps that will prevent him from ever being in a situation in which the sin could be repeated or temptation arise. Needless to say, that is a most traditional and careful approach to the problem, which emphasizes first and foremost the great risk of repetition after one has proved his weakness, and taking the most careful measures to make repetition impossible in practice.

Together with this suggestion, the Ashkenazi Hasidim mention another way: to prove to oneself and to God that one can return to the same situation in which one previously failed and transgressed, but this time successfully overcome one's desires and refrain from sinning.[29] According to this approach, a person has to return to the same place and the same set of circumstances and prove that he has overcome spiritually the inclination to sin. It is obvious that this second approach emphasizes the spiritual aspect of the sin, by demanding that the repentant prove he does not repeat the transgression merely because he does not have the opportunity, but because he has overcome the wish to do so in a spiritual manner.

After Rabbi Eleazar described this course of behavior of the repentant, he stated: "But this form of repentance is not practiced any more,[30] and he and others deal with it only briefly. It is not difficult to imagine the ethical dilemma that Rabbi Eleazar and others faced when discussing this spiritual way of proving one's success in repenting. If a Jew follows the first way and takes upon himself prohibitions that will make it impossible for him to repent his transgression, then, though he does not achieve a very high spiritual status, he is quite safe from any repetition of the sin. But if the other way is recommended by the teachers of ethics, what about those who will try it, and fail? If a person returns to the place and set of circumstances in which he had committed a sin, and repeats it, this time it is much worse, because retrospectively it would mean that he has committed it intentionally and in a premeditated way, willingly setting up the situation for the repetition of a crime he had committed once before. The responsibility will, at least to some extent, rest with the teacher, who encouraged him to do so. No wonder that Rabbi Eleazar does not emphasize or recommend this way to his readers; the reward might be great indeed, but the risk involved is enormous, especially when one is writing a popular work for the use of the masses.

This is the basic conflict between the orthodox, moderate, and careful approach to ethics and the adventurous way, in which great risks are taken in order to achieve maximal spiritual rewards. This is also evident in the Ashkenazi Hasidic hesitation concerning the recommendation that a person who does not have a strong urge to commit a certain transgression should encourage it by artificial means and thus will be able to prove his spiritual powers by overcoming it.[31]

The classical problem in this context in Ashkenazi Hasidic ethical literature is whether one should be encouraged to face the crusaders when they raid a town and demand that all Jews convert to Christianity, refuse conversion, and die on *kidush ha-shem*; or whether, whenever possible, one should hide and avoid the cruel choice? If one hides, he gives up the great opportunity of achieving supreme righteousness and the highest possible status in heaven. But if one faces the crusaders and fails the test, he will become the worst possible transgressor, and lose any chance of escaping everlasting punishment. In the works of the Ashkenazi Hasidim it is evident that their hearts were set on the adventurous way of taking risks in order to achieve the maximum in religious life. But the caution of teachers to the masses forbade them from clearly expressing this preference lest they lead simple Jews who do not have the spiritual strength to succeed in such a difficult test into a sinful and wicked life.

There can be no doubt that the Ashkenazi Hasidim succeeded in presenting a system of ethics that was based on a spiritual approach to religious life and put emphasis almost exclusively on the inner, emotional side of religious experience, even though they did not neglect the performance of the physical, external religious demands and did not offer any way by which they could be minimized in importance. The price they paid for this achievement was the negation of the notion that God's goodness can be found in his demands from man. The demands are harsh and difficult, their purpose being to overcome man's human inclinations and prepare him for the final test, the complete sacrifice of man's humanity for the sake of God—*kidush ha-shem*.

VI

The theology of the Ashkenazi Hasidim introduced into medieval Jewish thought the idea of a multilevel deity, each aspect of which had its own function in the divine system of providence for the world. In this way they probably preceded the kabbalistic system of the ten divine emanations (the *sefirot*) by a few years. But there is a significant difference between the multiaspect Ashkenazi Hasidic divine world and the kabbalistic one. The Hasidim gave detailed (though nonrationalistic) reasons for their theological conclusions, while the kabbalists described the "tree" of divine emanations as an ancient tradition that cannot be explained, and the functional differences between the various aspects of the Godhead as the result of exegesis and homiletical hermeneutics. In other words, in the Ashkenazi Hasidic esoteric literature one can easily discern the reasons for their theological conclusions, while in the first work of the Kabbalah, the book *Bahir*, the conclusions are presented first, and the reasons for the structure of ten emanations are traditional rather than theological.

When the Ashkenazi Hasidim differentiate between two aspects of divine revelation, this distinction is not contained in the abstract theological realm, but has clear consequences in the field of everyday ethics. The division between the hidden God and His immanence and the revealed divine glory and its immanence is meaningful in terms of their practical instructions of social ethics.

The revealed aspect of the hidden, supreme Godhead is the act of creation. The Ashkenazi Hasidim, when presenting the distinction between the revealed and the hidden God, always refer to the higher aspect by the title *ha-bore*, the Creator.[32] Needless to say, every rationalistic philosopher would immediately point out that a divine power cannot be at the same time both hidden and revealed, and therefore the supreme Godhead, which is eternal, unchanged, and unchanging, cannot be described as the creator. The act of creation, the decision to make something out of nothing, is the most momentous change in the divine world, and its perpetrator cannot be described as unchanging. But the Ashkenazi Hasidim were not rationalistic philosophers; their esoteric theology insists on this paradox, according to which the supreme, unchanging Godhead is the Creator.

They do adhere, however, to rationalistic reasoning when describing the divine immanence of the supreme, hidden Godhead. According to them, as mentioned above, this immanence is to be found in every realm of existence, in every part of the created world, in an even, steady, and unchanging way; divine immanence of this kind is to be found even in the heart of evil, sin, or dirt. Their idea is that this divine immanence is so supreme in nature that it cannot be affected by the specific characteristics of the elements within which it resides. It can be stated paradoxically, that this immanence is so transcendent that even though it is everywhere, it touches nothing and is touched by nothing. The whole existence is inside the Creator, and the Creator is inside everything; but they do not touch and do not affect each other.

The Creator is the source of all the laws that govern the creation. The rules that govern nature and society, the celestial powers, and the earthly forces, were all decided by the Godhead when the creation occurred. These laws are unchanging, and they reflect the main purpose of creation: to test the righteous, to present them with the harshest possible obstacles, so that if they do adhere to the divine demands and live righteously, they will have overcome so many difficulties to be worthy of the title "righteous," and the world will continue to exist because of their achievements. This idea denotes that the Creator is not only a hidden God, but that His goodness is completely hidden. The laws by which He created the world do not reflect His intrinsic benevolence, for were He to express His goodness in the process of creation, no difficulties would exist, everything would be easy, and righteousness would lose its meaning because no effort was needed in order to achieve it. Creation in this way would not produce human beings, torn by their evil desires, but another set of angels, pure of all uncleanliness and wickedness. The world would have no reason to exist; creation would be negated because of the revelation of the Godhead's benevolence. Therefore, His goodness must be hidden behind the harshness of the laws of creation, the laws by which nature, society, and man are governed.

The lower, revealed divine power is the *kavod*, the divine glory. The glory is not eternal, and therefore not unchanging. It is an emanation from the Godhead, but while its upper "face" is a part of the Godhead, its lower "face" can be seen by the prophets and the righteous in certain circumstances. The physical, anthropomorphical descriptions of God found in the Bible, the Talmud, and the works of the ancient Jewish mystics of the talmudic period, the Hekhalot and Merkabah literature, all refer to the divine glory. Because it is revealed, it can assume a form, and its forms may change from one occasion to the other.

The glory is also immanent within creation, but not in the abstract, unchanging way of the Creator. It is present where it chooses to be revealed, and only in holy and clean places. The idea of revelation and the idea of divine immanence are united in this description of the presence of the divine glory. This is an immanence by choice, and not by necessity, and it is not governed by abstract, eternal laws, but chosen in every occasion by the wish of the divine glory.

These two levels of divine forces and divine immanence correspond to the two levels of ethical behavior and achievement in the Ashkenazi Hasidic system. The intrinsic goodness of the Creator is hidden; the goodness of the glory is revealed and present in the world when it chooses to manifest it. The presence of the goodness of the divine glory enables the righteous to overcome the harsh laws of creation, to break the deterministic rules that make righteousness impossible in this evil world, and to change the fate decreed by the Godhead into a more benevolent one, which enables the *hasid* to express his wish to serve God fully and faithfully.

A clear example of this rather unusual way of thinking can be found in the Ashkenazi Hasidic concepts of astrology and divine decrees. According to *Sefer Hasidim*, as well as the esoteric works of Rabbi Judah the Pious,[33] everything a man will do is decided before he is born. How long he will live, whether he will be rich or poor, whom he will marry, his children, his occupation, and all the other details that shape human life are decreed. But this is not all. The divine decrees concerning every individual include his thoughts and intentions, how many of them will be good and how many evil. Vivid descriptions in Rabbi Judah's works, especially in a treatise dedicated to the nature and function of the angels,[34] tell how hosts of angels of various classes come out of heaven and direct the smallest, most mundane act of every individual, including his innermost feelings and thoughts. Rabbi Judah describes how angels position themselves just outside the ears of a sleeping man, and in the early morning, when sleep is light, they murmur into his ears whatever they were instructed to convey. The drowsy man cannot distinguish between his original, autonomous thoughts and wishes and those planted in his mind by these angels. In this way God's decrees are conveyed to the world and shape it according to the grand design of the creation.

But which is the divine power behind these decrees? There is no doubt that the Ashkenazi Hasidim saw their origin with the Creator himself, the supreme Godhead, the source of all the laws that govern creation. These decrees are not only whispered to a sleeping man; they are also written in the heavens themselves, in the stars. Astrology, according to them, does not reveal the independent influence of the stars; it only reflects divine decrees. The prophecy of the stars is true not because the celestial lights decide human fate, but because God chose to write his decisions in the constellations. Similarly, every person has a spiritual, astral double (*zelem*),[35] which receives the divine decrees and reflects them even before they "reach" the earth and the material body of the individual. Thus, when a person is about to die, his *zelem* can be seen in certain circumstances as headless; the divine decree has been enacted already concerning the astral being, and the same fate will soon reach the material body of that person. It is God's decree that is revealed both by the stars and by the astral beings, reflecting the Creator's overall design for the universe.

This is a system that expresses deep belief in predestination, and its attitude toward human fate is deterministic. Man cannot influence his position in the world; everything has been decided long ago by the Creator, written in the stars, and reflected in the fate of the astral body. This fate, as stated above, includes not only the external circumstances of the individual, but also his feelings, wishes, and thoughts, and thereby also his religious attitude. Righteousness, in this system, is something that cannot be attained unless God has decreed so. But if God has decided that a certain person will be righteous, how can he be otherwise? And if righteousness means the overcoming of great hardships and trials, this cannot be real righteousness, because if it is the result of God's decree it cannot be negated, and therefore no overcoming of difficulties is needed; a person will be righteous because he has to be, and not because of his religious choice and his personal efforts in overcoming the trials before him. There is, no doubt, a most serious theological and religious problem present here, which had to be solved by the Hasidim.

Another aspect of the same problem is that of divine justice. If all man does throughout his life is enact predestined divine decrees, what is the meaning of religious reward and punishment? It is God Himself who has decided that a person will commit a sin or perform a charitable deed; let Him reward or punish Himself. Man was nothing but the external instrument for the performance of that good or evil deed, without his independent personality taking any part in the decision whether to choose the good or bad path. Without a choice, religious life loses all its meaning, and divine justice seems to be absent from the world.

The Ashkenazi Hasidim solved this problem by the paradox of double revelation and double divine immanence.[36] The deterministic decrees are those of the supreme Godhead, the Creator. They do not leave any place for free choice and for the expression of righteousness. The harsh decisions are written in the skies and in the fate of the astral being which accompanies every individual. But the Godhead expects at least some people to negate His decrees and become righteous in spite of the astrological commands and the whispers of the angels. A person can, though certainly not in extreme cases, overcome the divine decrees and become righteous in spite of the deterministic fate imposed on him from the moment he was born. God expects the righteous to deny His designs, prove that man can do the impossible, and, paradoxically, serve and obey God by refusing His harsh predestined fate. Righteousness is, according to this system, an overcoming of God's wishes by the worshiper in order to conform to God's true, inner wishes, which desire that man shall not yield to the external laws of nature and society, but shall express his love and fear of God in spite of the circumstances, created by God Himself, which seem to forbid it.

Righteousness is the victory of the exception over the law. According to law, there is no possibility of achieving righteousness. The way the human body and soul were designed, the way nature torments man, the way society treats the faithful—all these make the laws that govern existence inimical to the achievement of the supreme religious goal. But God expects man to overcome his own and his society's nature, to deny the decrees written in the stars, and to be righteous in spite of all the hardships. The miracles worked by the divine glory, and the revelations inspired by it, confirm the possibility of exceptions to the divine decrees.

Ashkenazi Hasidic ethics thus become part of the realm of the miraculous which is the realm of the divine glory's immanence. The achievement of righteousness means breaking the laws of nature, of the human body and soul, and of human history and society. This is what God expects of the *hasid*, even though the laws by which he created the world are intended to make this almost impossible. Only the presence of the divine glory contains an element of divine encouragement toward the attainment of the state of righteousness. The act of *kidush ha-shem* is the fullest expression of this miraculous overcoming of the natural laws and the full adherence to the hidden wishes of the Creator.

This attitude enables us to explain a central aspect of Ashkenazi Hasidic ethics which is closely connected to the mystical element in their system. When the subject of the love of God is described in *Sefer Hasidim*, we find a clear warning stated by the author: love should not become the dominant force in the relationship between man and God, because love breeds a feeling of intimacy and laxity, which might lead the faithful into neglecting the performance of his religious and ethical duties, believing that as God and he are so close to each other, there is no doubt that he will be forgiven for minor occasional transgressions. Therefore love of God should be interwoven into a more complex pattern, in which the dominant force is that of the fear of God, which means, according to the Hasidim, the fear of disobeying God.[37]

On the other hand, we find in *Sefer Hasidim* and in the works of Rabbi Eleazar of Worms a completely different description of the love of God.[38] In these paragraphs, the love of God is all-consuming; a man is completely absorbed in it and becomes spiritually removed from his family and his society. His feelings toward God are described in erotic terms, the metaphor used being that of a youth's orgasm. This is a description of an intense mystical relationship, in which the warnings and reservations presented in other descriptions are completely forgotten.

Is this a contradiction, or does the difference between these texts signify a difference in the religious meaning of the love of God? It seems to me that the double-immanence system of the Ashkenazi Hasidim can explain this phenomenon. The careful attitude of an element of love covered by layers of fear of God is the one demanded toward the Godhead, the Creator, the giver of the Torah and the commandments and the designer of the natural and social laws of this world. The intense mystical love, presented in erotic terms, is the attitude that the righteous can achieve toward the revealed divine glory. It is impossible to imagine a close relationship between man and the Creator; but it is possible toward the glory, if man has risen to the necessary supreme religious level, and if the glory chose to become close to him. Man can never be more than a humble servant to the Creator; he can achieve a close relationship with the divine glory, a relationship equated with erotic love.

The Ashkenazi Hasidim presented medieval Jewry with a most demanding and strict system of ethics. It is very doubtful that this system could have been accepted if it had been intended to serve only the remote, transcendent Creator, who brought forth the harsh laws of nature and presented man with all the hardships that prevent him from achieving righteousness. It is precisely the mystical element in the Ashkenazi Hasidic system that made their ethics acceptable, by presenting the possibility of a closer, bilateral relationship with the revealed divine glory. The mystical element was thus the human element that enriched the spiritual world of the Ashkenazi Hasidim and brought their extreme ethical demands into the realm of the spiritually possible and desirable.

4

MYSTICAL ETHICS IN
SIXTEENTH-CENTURY SAFED

I

MYSTICAL IDEAS AND symbols served as a hidden force behind the
ethical teachings of the kabbalists in Gerona and the Ashkenazi
Hasidim in the Rhineland, but most medieval mystics insisted on
a separation between their ethical works and their mystical writings. Ethics was directed toward the Jewish public as a whole,
while mysticism was an esoteric subject, the domain of a close
circle of the initiated. This strict separation remained almost intact
for three centuries. But in the sixteenth century the distinction
vanished, and Jewish ethics and Jewish mysticism were fused
together into one system of religious life, which brought about a
revolution in Jewish culture. This dramatic change occurred in the
small town of Safed in Upper Galilee, which was the scene of some
of the most profound developments in the history of Jewish
thought.

The dominant element in the establishment of the great cultural
center in sixteenth-century Safed was the refugees who reached it
following the catastrophe of the expulsion of the Jews from Spain in
1492. This expulsion was a traumatic experience for the Jewish
people for two reasons. The first was the actual destruction, almost
overnight, of the largest, centuries-old center of Jewish life and
culture in Europe. Scores of Jewish communities, which for many
centuries produced Jewish scholars, poets, philosophers, and

halakhists, vanished at the stroke of a monarch's pen. The most firmly established Jewish families in Europe, which for centuries were the focus of the financial and political power of European Jewry, became scattered refugees. This dramatic fall of the most magnificent achievement of the Jews in medieval Europe shook Judaism, and the realization of exilic experience, which had become dormant during the long prosperity of Spanish Jewry, suddenly became the dominant element in Jews' perception of the historical existence of Judaism in the world. After this destruction, nothing was safe, nothing was certain, in Jewish life; and a theological explanation of this tragedy was necessary.[1]

The second traumatic experience of this period was the result of so many of the Jews of Spain not going into exile, but remaining in Spain (and later in Portugal) as new converts to the Catholic faith, the Marranos.[2] This phenomenon, starting when the period of persecutions began in 1391, became so widespread that to many Jews at that time it seemed that the higher classes of Jewish society, the rich and the educated, had almost unanimously chosen conversion over exile. It became customary to compare these converts to the Ashkenazi Jews who preferred being massacred by the crusaders or committing suicide to converting in Germany in the eleventh and twelfth centuries. It seemed as if Spanish Jewry was much weaker, when the terrible test came, than Ashkenazi Jewry had been three centuries before. The leaders and intellectuals among the exiled Spanish Jews began to seek an explanation for this disturbing phenomenon.

Jewish philosophy was regarded by many of the thinkers of the period as the main cultural force that should be blamed for Jewish weakness in the face of the choice between conversion and exile.[3] It seemed to them that the spiritualization of religious life, in the manner preached by the rationalists, and the allegorization of the *mitzvot* made it easier for Jewish intellectuals to downgrade the importance of the external expressions of Jewish worship, and thus to make the external conversion less meaningful. One can worship the true God in his heart in a church as well as in a synagogue, if the *mitzvot* have no inherent religious meaning at least as far as their material, apparent side is concerned. Whether this argument is true or not, the fact remains that the prestige of Jewish philosophy declined dramatically after the expulsion from Spain, and in the following centuries its impact on Jewish culture declined and in some places almost vanished. The world of Jewish thought was waiting for new ideas and new interpretations of Jewish tradition, which would take into account the recent upheavals, both physical and spiritual, of the expulsion from Spain.

Besides these two major forces—the new realization of exilic uncertainties and the decline of Jewish philosophy—another problem faced sixteenth-century Jews: the search for a substitute for the destroyed center of Jewish culture in Spain. Another center had to be found to replace the most prosperous and important center that had been so ruthlessly eliminated. The small Jewish community at Safed, which never reached the size of one of the major cities in Spain as far as Jewish population was concerned, assumed the task not only of offering a new meaning to Jewish existence in exile and a new interpretation of Jewish tradition to replace Jewish philosophy, but also of establishing a new center of Jewish culture that would fill the place of the destroyed one in Spain.[4]

It is an irony of history that not only allowed the Jewish scholars in Safed to have such dreams of grandeur, absurd from any practical point of view, but also allowed this unbelievable enterprise to succeed. Safed became in the sixteenth century the main center of Jewish creativity, and its achievements had a tremendous impact on the development of Judaism in the centuries that followed. Safed gave to Judaism, in two generations of an intensely creative period, the most important elements of Jewish culture in the seventeenth, eighteenth, and nineteenth centuries, when the center moved to Eastern Europe. The basic pillars upon which the structure of Jewish culture in Eastern Europe rested were built in Safed in the sixteenth century.

Jewish law in the modern period, to this very day, is based on the *Shulḥan Aruch*, the work of Rabbi Joseph Karo of Safed. Jewish homiletical literature, which played a major role in East European Hebrew culture, achieved its peak in Safed in the works of Rabbi Moshe Alsheikh, the great homilist-exegete who was the most quoted authority in East European and Mediterranean Jewish homiletics. And as far as ideology and theology are concerned, Safed gave the Jewish world the teachings of Rabbi Isaac Luria Ashkenazi, known by the acronym ha-Ari ("The Lion"), whose mystical symbolism became the basis of all subsequent traditional Jewish thinking, from the heretical followers of the messiah Shabatai Zevi to the pietistic disciples of the founder of modern Hasidim, Rabbi Israel Baal Shem Tov, the renowned Besht. Moreover, in Safed a unity was reached between mystical theology and ethical behavior which has shaped the way of life of generations of Jews to this very day. The following brief survey is intended to present this unique phenomenon in Jewish history, with an emphasis on the development of mystical ethics.

II

The historian of ideas usually looks for the origins of a new idea in the works of philosophers and theologians, knowing that, in time, their most profound and potent insights spread out from their birthplace in intellectual speculation and can be found in more and more popular works, until they are included among the basic concepts of a society and determine its everyday way of life. In Safed, so it seems, the process was reversed, and we find several of the key concepts of mystical theology and ethics being enacted in the way of life of the community before the theoretical and theological formulation was written down. It seems that the great mystics of Safed were not only the leaders of this community, but followed its new customs and ethical emphases and created their systems according to the norms that had ruled Safed before them.

Lurianic mystical theology insisted, for instance, on every individual's participation, in the most active way, in the process of bringing forth a redemption.[5] Yet, nearly two generations before Luria presented his system to his handful of disciples, we find in Safed—for the first time in medieval Jewish history—a collective effort to enhance the coming of the redemption. This is the great controversy concerning the ordination of rabbis, the *semichah*.

According to Jewish law, based on the stories of Moses in the Book of Exodus, a Jewish rabbi must be ordained by his teacher, who must himself be an ordained rabbi; thus an uninterrupted succession of teachers and disciples, through which the oral law is transmitted, leads from Moses to the present. This law was preserved throughout ancient times, sometimes with great sacrifices.[6] In the Middle Ages the chain was broken, and the rabbis ordained then were not regarded as truly connected to the Mosaic source of authority. Medieval rabbis, therefore, did not have the same powers as the ancient, fully ordained rabbis. Ordination would resume, according to the common belief, when the messiah would come and reinstitute it.

How will the messiah renew the broken chain of the *semichah*? The most authoritative answer to this question was given by Maimonides in his code of Jewish law, the *Mishneh Torah*.[7] According to him, the messiah himself will not do it (for then he would be as great as Moses, and Maimonides was careful not to open any avenue for a change in Jewish law even in messianic times), but a meeting of all the rabbis of Eretz Israel will nominate one among them as ordained, and this first ordained rabbi will have the power to fully ordain others.

A meeting of the rabbis of Safed was convened according to this ruling and they elected the best scholar among them, Rabbi Jacob Berav, the teacher of Rabbi Joseph Karo, to be the first truly ordained rabbi.[8] But Safed did not include all the rabbis then living in Eretz Israel; there was another great and learned community, that of Jerusalem. Rabbi Jacob Berav tried to convince the rabbis of Jerusalem to join the venture of the rabbis of Safed, and thus make it fully conform with Maimonides's ruling. The rabbis of Jerusalem, however, rejected the offer and announced their clear opposition to the whole idea.

A long controversy ensued, encased in strictly legal and halakhic terminology, but behind that a deep difference is apparent. The rabbis of Safed believed that the redemption was very close, and that it was the duty of everyone to support the messianic process by individual and communal activity. The rabbis of Jerusalem opposed this view, believing that nothing should be done until the actual appearance of the messiah; passive waiting and strict adherence to traditional Jewish laws were all that could be done until the messiah came and told the people what to do.

The opposition of the Jerusalem rabbis should, so it seems, have put an end to the Safed enterprise, for clearly the ruling of Maimonides was not followed to its end. Yet we know that the practice of ordination continued in Safed for the next four generations. Among the ordained rabbis was, first and foremost, Rabbi Joseph Karo, the author of the *Shulhan Aruch*, and we have every reason to suppose that the fact that this halakhic work was composed by an ordained rabbi contributed to its unique influence and prestige. Other ordained rabbis were Rabbi Moshe Alsheikh, the great preacher and exegete, and Rabbi Hayim Vital, the great disciple of Rabbi Isaac Luria, whose works were the avenue by which Lurianic teachings spread to the whole Jewish world.

The theological and mystical basis for immediate messianic activity was supplied by Luria nearly fifty years after Rabbi Jacob Berav's messianic venture; but the atmosphere in Safed had already established modes of behavior in the same direction even though the systematic ideological basis was still missing. Acute messianic sentiments and expectations were not aroused by Luria in Safed; rather, he formulated in a systematic way an existing spiritual trend.

In a similar way, the idea of communal rather than individual responsibility, also one of the characteristics of Lurianic views, is described in Safed before the appearance of Luria. We have descriptions, for instance, of a Safed rabbi, Rabbi Abraham ha-Levi Beruchim, who used to go from house to house on Sabbath eve to check whether all cooking had been finished and all fires put out; if he found food still in the lighted oven, he would confiscate it for the poorhouse. He also used to get up in the middle of the night and call for all the people in the town to rise and study and worship, expressing their sorrow for the destruction of the temple.[9] According to the information included in letters that have been preserved, the people accepted this intrusion into their private religious practice, and accepted the norm of communal responsibility before God, through which the delinquency of one person can harm the efforts of the whole group. In this and other ways Safed conceived itself to be a Holy Community (*kehilat kodesh*), with special obligations for the nation as a whole, and as a result each member of this community had the obligation to accept the demands of his neighbors and share in their religious enterprise.

It is quite possible that this unique attitude was also based on messianic motives. If the people of Israel as a whole cannot strictly follow the demands of both the halakhah and Jewish ethics—a situation which, if it were possible, would undoubtedly bring about the coming of the redemption— then it might suffice if one community carried out in an extreme way all the ritualistic and ethical precepts of Judaism. This community, serving as a representative of the people as a whole, could bring about the coming of the messiah. Safed set out to be such a representative community, feeling that the fate of the whole people and the whole world rested on its shoulders.

Another aspect of the activity of Rabbi Abraham ha-Levi Beruchim reveals this attitude in a more extreme way: his concept of repentance. According to contemporary sources, Rabbi Abraham used to wander through the streets, calling upon the people to repent. He would then gather a group of people around him and lead them to the synagogue, where he would place himself in a sack, close it, and order the people to throw big stones at him. Sometimes he would strip naked and roll over poisonous thorns until all his flesh was burning. He would then announce that this was the way of the truly repentant, and that everyone should follow in his footsteps. Another story from this period is about an anonymous repentant who used to sneak into a sack at midnight, roll to the door of the synagogue, and stay there, without food and without anyone seeing him until the next midnight, to express his adherence to the new norms of repentant life.

The terminology used in the descriptions of this behavior concerning repentance clearly denotes the influence of Ashkenazi Hasidic ideas concerning repentance. The medieval pietists conserved in their ethical works the system of *teshuvat ha-katuv*, "repentance according to the biblical verses," by which a person guilty of the worst social and religious crimes, like murder or fornication, was to undertake upon himself extreme tortures similar to the sentence of death that biblical law demands in such cases. It is quite certain that the Ashkenazi Hasidim never used these methods, but the scholars of Safed adopted the system described in the earlier works of Rabbi Eleazar of Worms and turned them into the actual everyday behavior of those adopting the title and way of life of the repentant, the *baal-teshuvah*

There is, however, a deep difference between the Ashkenazi Hasidic system and that of the Safed rabbis. The medieval pietists described these tortures as undertaken by a person guilty of the greatest of sins. One should not conclude that Rabbi Abraham ha-Levi and his followers in Safed were indeed guilty of murder and fornication. The radical new idea that prevailed in Safed was that penitence should be a way of life, completely independent of the individual's sins. Even if one had not committed any grave sin, somebody else, in another time or place, certainly had. Religious life, as a struggle toward cosmic redemption, was not regarded as an individual matter, but rather as a collective duty, in which the extra efforts of one righteous person could atone for the transgressions of somebody else, even someone unknown to him. It is as if God does not observe and reward the actions of each person, but has a collective account for the nation as a whole. Every sin, therefore, hurts the status of everybody, and every righteous deed supports the religious standing of everybody else. The nation as a whole, beyond geographic and temporal boundaries, is responsible together before God. When this attitude is adopted, repentance cannot remain the realm of an individual accounting for the individual's sins. There can be no end to religious efforts, because there is no doubt that somewhere or sometime there exists a sinner whose transgressions are being atoned for by the efforts of the rabbi in the synagogue in Safed.

Several sources concerning Safed in this period indicate the appearance of a new practice: the organization of groups of scholars dedicated to a repentant way of life. These groups convened once a week, at which time each person would describe his deeds and confess to his sins, and all the members would participate in discussing everybody else's behavior, supporting each other in the difficult task they had undertaken. No such practices are known to us before their appearance in sixteenth-century Safed.

This and other new concepts of religious behavior are found in our sources independent of any systematic ethical or theological formulation. A new mystical ethical system was emerging in Safed, deeply connected with messianic expectations, before the great mystics associated with this town presented their works of mystical ethics. The appearance of mystical works combining kabbalistic symbolism and ethical norms only strengthened this process, causing its impact to spread outside of Safed and to influence the way of life of modern traditional Jewry.

III

The greatest mystic of Safed prior to the appearance of Isaac Luria was Rabbi Moses Cordovero, one of the most important kabbalistic authors of all time. Though many volumes of his works have been printed, many remain in manuscript. Only recently a project for the publication of his magnum opus, *Or Yakar*, the commentary on the *Zohar* (the great mystical work written in Spain in the thirteenth century), has begun, with a dozen folio volumes published to date. [10] His best-known and highly influential kabbalistic work is the *Pardes Rimonim*, "A Pomegranate Orchard," one of the few classics of the Kabbalah. In this book, as in others, Cordovero did not regard himself as an original mystical thinker; he saw himself as a collector, interpreter, and organizer in a systematic way of the teachings of previous kabbalists, especially the *Zohar*. The body of his works can be viewed as a systematic summary of the Kabbalah up to his time, and the *Pardes*, especially, is presented as a subject by subject, step by step, presentation of the Zoharic concepts of the Godhead, the divine *sefirot*, the celestial powers, and the earthly processes. It even includes one chapter (number 23) that is an alphabetic dictionary of the most important Zoharic and kabbalistic symbols and terms, as explained by Cordovero.

Most of Cordovero's works are voluminous, detailed, and exhaustive. But one of his most important and influential books is a very small treatise, hardly twenty pages long, called *Tomer Devorah*, "The Palm Tree of Deborah." [11] This is Cordovero's one and only treatise dedicated to the subject of ethics. Though it is brief, its ideas helped revolutionize the relationship between Jewish mysticism and Jewish ethics.

The subject of "The Palm Tree of Deborah" is a process known in the history of religions as *imitatio dei*, expressing the idea that in order to achieve the highest degree of the religious life one should not only follow the demands of God as expressed in his revealed words, but also imitate in his behavior divine patterns and processes. This idea can be found in the *Zohar* itself, and Cordovero both quotes and follows Zoharic passages when presenting his system. But this small treatise is the first in which a systematic presentation of everyday ethical behavior is completely dependent on the idea that one's deeds should reflect the inner structure of the deity, as found in kabbalistic symbolism.

Cordovero divided this book into ten chapters, arranged according to the structure of the ten *sefirot*, the ten divine powers or hypostases in the kabbalistic world view. The ten chapters do not follow strictly the ten *sefirot*; the first two are dedicated to the same supreme power, the "supreme crown" (*keter elyon*), the most hidden and sublime of the aspects of Godhead in the Kabbalah. To this power the talmudic thirteen "attributes of mercy" are connected, [12] and Cordovero discussed each of them in detail. The remaining chapters deal with the lower nine *sefirot*.

Although "The Palm Tree of Deborah" is a work about ethical behavior, its actual instructions are traditional, and very often elementary and mundane. Cordovero insists in the various chapters on man's need to study and to teach, to lead those dependent on him charitably and wisely, to dedicate his efforts to charity and assistance to the needy, and other minimal actions of social ethics (though concerning repentance he demands, characteristically, that all one's life should be dedicated to this religious value). What is new in this treatise is Cordovero's systematic connection between the various divine attributes and manifestations and these social and ritualistic actions. If one follows these norms, says Cordovero, one becomes identified with the divine power which is associated with that deed, and thus the righteous may imitate God's ways and become connected to him. It is not the system of ethics presented in the work that is meaningful; it is the mystical idea that by following simple, everyday ethical commandments a person can participate in the inner developments within the Godhead, and become a part of the united divine and earthly divine providence.

As stated above, Jewish ethics in the Middle Ages and modern times is not concerned so much with the problem of what should be done in a certain set of circumstances, as with the question of why should one follow the ethical demands. To this question Cordovero presents the first clear and unambiguous mystical answer: ethical behavior should be adopted and followed not only because God says so, but because God is so; one should conform not only to the divine laws, but to the divine nature. The righteous, thus, is not only an obedient servant of God, but an imitator of His essence, and therefore a part of the divine system as a whole. Mystical ascent and everyday ethics are fused into one, and the highest achievement of communion with God is attained by following the most mundane and elementary demands of social ethics. This is a revolution not in the behavior of the righteous, but in the meaning of this behavior. After this treatise had been published and accepted, the teachers of Jewish ethics could make use of all the intricate symbolism of Kabbalah in order to set forth the path toward righteous behavior. The distinction between an ethical work and a mystical one was erased, and a whole literature came into being, the literature of mystical ethics, which dominated Jewish thought during the next three centuries.

Cordovero's treatise spread very swiftly, both as an independent book and as part of other works. *Shnei Luhot ha-Berit*, for instance, the influential ethical study by Isaiah ha-Levi Horowitz, who lived in Poland and Safed at the end of the sixteenth century and the beginning of the seventeenth, includes the whole "Palm Tree of Deborah." Many homiletical works written in Eastern Europe adopted its main ideas in greater or less detail. One of the most important ways by which Cordovero's message spread was through the works of his disciples, especially Rabbi Eliyahu de Vidas's *Reshit Hochmah* ("The Beginning of Wisdom"), a detailed and extensive work on spiritual ethics, which was the first book of kabbalistic ethics to be printed and which became an extremely popular book. Because of its length, abbreviated versions were written, adding to its influence. Cordovero and his disciples laid the foundation for the fusion of Jewish ethics and Jewish mysticism in Safed, a process that Isaac Luria developed in his revolutionary new kabbalistic system.

The appearance of Cordoverian kabbalistic ethics in Safed, based to a very large extent on the teachings of the *Zohar* and other earlier mystical works, provides a suitable opportunity to study the nature of the mystical system of ethics presented by the kabbalists, and to try to understand their addition of a mystical dimension to Jewish ethics, before we turn to the overused mystical-ethical system later developed in Safed by Isaac Luria.

IV

The early kabbalists, like the Jewish philosophers and the Ashkenazi Hasidim, were faced with the problem of the spiritual meaning of the material commandments that constitute the basis of Jewish religious practice. While many philosophers chose to regard the *mitzvot* as allegories for theological and philosophical truths, and the Ashkenazi Hasidim found a spiritual dimension in the efforts demanded for the performance of the *mitzvot* in the face of hardships, the kabbalists chose a different way, a mystical one: the conception of the commandments as symbols.

The mystical symbol is different in character from the symbol appearing in literature and everyday speech. While the ordinary use of this term usually includes both the symbol and the symbolized (as Ibsen's Nora is a symbol of the struggle for women's liberation), the mystical symbol cannot be followed by an explanation or categorization, because it represents the maximum that can be expressed in human language concerning a divine truth that cannot be explained in any earthly way. The mystic, who believes that truth transcends human experience, senses, speech, and intellect, does not believe that the ordinary human means of communication can denote divine truth. Mystical truth can be hinted at by words, but nothing can be added to this vague hint; it can be understood, actually, only by other mystics who have a glimpse of the transcendent truth that is hidden behind the symbol.

The concept of the mystical symbol is most clearly presented by the mystic's concept of the nature of the Bible. On the one hand, the sacred book is written in ordinary, everyday words, their meaning deriving from human sensual and intellectual experience. On the other hand, as the Bible is divine revelation, it must denote the complete, mystical truth, which cannot be expressed in human language. This contradiction is resolved by the understanding that the divine truth in the Bible is given by means of mystical symbols. The nonmystic reading the Bible believes that the words convey laws and stories, history and ethics, expressed in ordinary human terms. Only the mystic knows that this level of expression is merely the external, superficial layer of the Word of God. Behind it hides mystical truth, and the connection between these two levels is one of symbolism.

Biblical symbolism cannot be explained and revealed, because, when choosing His words, God expressed in a symbolic way the maximum that can be expressed in human language. Only mystical experience or insight can give some hint of the truth that lies beyond the sensual and intellectual terminology of the Bible. The mystic reading the Bible therefore reads a completely different book from the one read by the nonmystic; he knows that the words are symbols, and because of his mystical experience he has a glimpse of the divine truth that is hinted at by the symbolical terms chosen by God.

What is true about biblical stories or historical narratives is doubly true concerning the large part of the Bible dedicated to religious laws and ethical instruction. Here not only are the words symbolic, but the deeds demanded of man, both ritualistic and ethical, carry symbolic meaning. Indeed, the reason for the divine demands of man can be known only symbolically. In this way the kabbalists achieved both a spiritualization of the religious laws and the ethical demands, and strict adherence to their performance.

The kabbalistic view of the commandments turned them into the expression of the maximum of divine revelation possible between God and man; they are the symbols of the hand of God reaching toward man and teaching him the very little that can be taught concerning the way a human being may try to participate in the divine scheme of things. The complete truth, and the place of each commandment in it, is completely hidden; it is mystical. But God, in His benevolence, provided man with some means of establishing contact—in a very remote way—with God. The Torah and the *mitzvot* included in it, both written and oral, the whole enormous body of Jewish commandments and ethical demands, are an edifice built of symbols, each of which and all of them together representing the maximum connection that is possible between the earthly and the divine, using material means.

The question of the "reasons" for the *mitzvot*, which bothered the philosophers, is thus completely removed in a kabbalistic system, not because they neglected it, but because they solved it. The kabbalists seem to have written more works on *ta'amey ha-mitzvot*, the explanations and reasons for the commandments, than did the Jewish philosophers. Since the second half of the thirteenth century such works were written by some of the greatest kabbalists, among them, for instance, Rabbi Moshe de Leon, the author of the *Zohar*. Even the *Zohar* itself includes a section dealing with these explanations. [13]

The kabbalistic *ta'amey ha-mitzvot*, however, are different from those of the philosophers in one cardinal way: the mystic who "explains" the commandments does not "reveal" the true, divine reason behind the *mitzvot*, as the philosopher tries to do. All he does is to substitute one set of symbols for the other. Instead of using the instructions of the halakhah, the actual demands for religious ritual and ethics, he transforms the commandment into the framework of the traditional symbolism of the *sefirot* and the divine processes of the kabbalists. For instance, where the halakhah, following the Torah, demands the building of a *sukkah* to live in during the days of the Festival of Sukkot, and defines exactly the way that this tabernacle should be built, the mystic explains: in this festival the feminine element of the divine world is married to the masculine part (the *Shekhinah*, which is the tenth divine emanation, is married to the sixth one, *Tiferet*). The *sukkah*, therefore, represents the bridal canopy for this conjugal occasion, and by building it according to all the halakhic specifications, one can participate in this momentous celestial occurrence.

Is this an "explanation"? It is not. Is it true that the *Shekhinah* marries the masculine part of the divine realm? Of course not. These are nothing but symbols, which, when taken as if they were human, earthly terms that have a literal meaning, do not convey anything. This picture of a divine wedding is a kabbalistic symbol that has no literal significance; only the mystic, who has had a glimpse of the mystical truth beyond human knowledge and sensory awareness, can have some inkling of the reality behind the symbols. The kabbalist writing "*ta'amey mitzvot*" is just changing one set of symbols for another, without bringing the symbols themselves nearer to their source in the divine realm.

Hence the great practical difference between the philosophical rationalistic meanings for the commandments and the mystical ones: one can try to achieve the rational end by using another way, not described by the halakhah, because he is in a position of knowing all the relevant facts and reasons. The mystic, however, does not know the "true" reasons, only the vague hints suggested by the symbols. All he can do, therefore, is to try to unite himself, as deeply and thoroughly as possible, with the divine symbol with which the Torah provides him. He cannot change any detail or suggest a new emphasis because he does not know the truth behind the symbols. Kabbalistic concepts of the commandments, there-fore, must be traditional; they may "explain" by offering another set of symbols, but they cannot change any halakhic detail, since these are symbols designed by divine omniscience and presented to man by divine benevolence.

In this way, the *mitzvot* become a material representation, in a symbolic way, of the most spiritual processes going on in the divine realm. The building of the *sukkah* is undoubtedly a material enterprise, but its significance—hinted at by the symbol but actually unknown and unknowable—is purely spiritual, since divine emanations and celestial powers are hidden behind it. Kabbalistic symbolism thus offered Judaism a most profound and imaginative way of achieving both strict adherence to orthodoxy and a revolutionary spiritualization of religious and ethical deeds.

Moses Cordovero's *Tomer Devorah*, and the other ethical works that his disciples and followers wrote, inserting the concept of *imitatio dei* into Jewish ethical literature and bringing it into every Jewish home through their popular works, thus made the kab-balistic symbolical conception of the commandments available not only to the closed circles of mystics but to the people as a whole. The new kabbalistic ethical literature did not teach its readers what to do; this they knew from halakhic and earlier ethical works. It taught their readers a new meaning for the traditional demands, denoting the vast significance that these symbols carried for the cosmos, for the Jewish people as a whole, and even, in a theurgic way, for the completeness of the divine realm itself.

The school of Cordovero made only the first step in this direction. The great, revolutionary change that made mystical ethics part of the culture of the whole Jewish people was based on a new set of symbols introduced into Judaism by Rabbi Isaac Luria Ashkenazi.

V

Unlike Rabbi Moses Cordovero, Isaac Luria did not intend his ideas to be published and become part of the everyday life and ethical behavior of the Jewish masses. Luria regarded his teachings as esoteric, and he himself never wrote a book, explaining that his ideas and pictures appear in such torrents that no thin pen can be used to present them. His disciple, Rabbi Hayim Vital, who outlived Luria by nearly forty years, dedicated all his efforts to writing Luria's teachings in books—which he kept secret. He forbade his colleagues and disciples to discuss Lurianic teachings with an outsider,[14] and legend has it that his books began to be disseminated after they were stolen from his house and copied while he was sick. A visitor to Safed in the early years of the seventeenth century, who heard and wrote many stories about Luria, was still very careful not to reveal any of the actual contents of his new Kabbalah.[15] Despite these attitudes of its founders, Lurianic theology became in subsequent generations almost the only basis of Jewish ethics, while even its dissemination and acceptance were the result of the new integration between Jewish mysticism and Jewish ethics.

Rabbi Isaac Luria Ashkenazi arrived in Safed in 1570, when he was thirty-six years old. His background and education, as well as his life before coming to Safed, are almost unknown and were mysterious even to his disciples. He died in a pestilence two years later, in 1572, after revealing his mystical mythology to a dozen close disciples. It is difficult to believe how far-reaching were the results of this brief interlude of two years in sixteenth-century Safed.

It is impossible in this brief book to give a detailed outline of Lurianic mysticism. Gershom Scholem and Isaiah Tishby have done this in their books. [16] We shall concentrate here only on those aspects that are directly related to the new fusion between mysticism and Jewish ethics which Lurianic mythology brought about.

The greatness of the Lurianic system is its direct and forceful responses to the most basic and existential problems that trouble religion and philosophy. Luria put in the heart of his mysticism the problems in the creation of the world and the creation of man, to which he gave the clearest answers to be found in Jewish mystical literature. He dealt with the problem that most troubled his generation: that of the reason for the exile of the people of Israel, a problem which the tragic results of the expulsion of the Jews from Spain made all the more acute. His treatment of the question of the origins and meaning of the existence of evil is the most penetrating in Jewish thought. And he succeeded in translating his answers into a practical religious and ethical system which every Jew, even if completely ignorant of Lurianic symbolism, could follow and fulfill.

Three powerful symbols, each denoting a mythological process within the Godhead, are at the heart of Lurianic Kabbalah: the symbols of the *tzimtzum*, the "contraction" of the Godhead; the *shevirah*, the "breaking" of the divine "vessels"; and the greatest of them, the symbol of the *tikkun*, the "mending" of the divine realm and the redemption.

The beginning of the process of creation in the realm of the supreme Godhead is described in the literature of the early Kabbalah, including the *Zohar*, as a positive event: the will to create, to express God's benevolence, was awakened within the Godhead, and the long process of emanation and creation began to unfold stage by stage. Luria, in the idea of the *tzimtzum*, postulated an earlier stage preceding the traditional ones: in order to create, the supreme Godhead, the *En Sof*, had to create an empty space in which the creation could be brought forth. The divine "light" of the Godhead was everywhere (actually, nowhere, because no place existed yet), and in order to create something "outside" the Godhead, such an "outside" had to be prepared.

The *tzimtzum* is the contraction of the Godhead into itself, away from a certain space which was thus emptied (called "tehiru," the Aramaic for "empty"). Thus, the first divine action in the history of the evolving cosmos was not a positive one but one of withdrawal: the Godhead had to forsake the *tehiru*, or even to exile itself from it, in order that the process of creation could be initiated. The *tzimtzum*, therefore, though positive in its intention, postulates divine exile as the beginning of all existence. Exile is no longer a human term, relating to the fate of the Jewish people; it is a mysterious process within the Godhead, which began long before the creation of man or of the people of Israel.

After the *tzimtzum*, Lurianic mythology seems to follow the old, traditional kabbalistic system. A line of divine light, called "the straight line" (*kav ha-yashar*), began to flow from the Godhead "outside" into the *tehiru* and assumed the shape of the world of the *sefirot*, the divine emanations pictured in the form of primordial man, *adam kadmon*. The divine creative force was expressing itself in the fullest manner, and divine lights created the "vessels," the external shapes of the *sefirot*, which give specific characteristics to each divine emanation and distinguish between it and the other powers. Into these "vessels" the full power of the Godhead was pouring its purest lights to fulfill the vessels and thus bring forth the divine emanations as intended in the supreme scheme of the process of creation.

At this crucial point a disaster occurred, a mythological event reminiscent of Manichaean gnostic mythology: the vessels were not powerful enough to hold the divine lights flowing into them, and they broke down. The "breaking of the vessels," the *shevirah*, occurred, bringing catastrophe and upheaval to the emerging system of the emanations. The lower vessels broke down and fell, the three highest emanations escaped but were damaged, and the *tehiru* was divided into two parts: the realm of the broken vessels, with many divine sparks clinging to them; and the upper realm, where the pure light of the Godhead escaped to preserve its purity from the mythological disaster.

The philosophical reasons behind this bizarre myth involve the Lurianic concepts of the reasons for the *tzimtzum* and the origin of the creation process, as well as the eternal problem of the source of evil. According to the most esoteric part of Lurianic teachings, revealed only after a meticulous study of the works of Luria's disciples by Gershom Scholem and Isaiah Tishby, the eternal Godhead before the beginning of the creation process was not completely united and of one nature. There were elements in it that were potentially (for nothing actually existed at that stage) different from the rest of the Godhead. The very purpose of the *tzimtzum* was to separate these different elements from the other divine lights.

When the Godhead initially contracted itself out of the empty space, something was left behind; the Lurianists use the metaphor of water clinging to the bucket after it has been emptied. This residue was called *reshimu*, the "impression" of the divine light that had been there before. This residue, according to Lurianic mythology, included in it those different elements that had previously been interwoven into the Godhead itself. After the *tzimtzum* they were separated into the *tehiru*, and thus the first task, the separation of different elements from the Godhead, was successfully accomplished.

The real reason for the emanation of the divine powers and the creation of the "primordial man" was the attempt to integrate these now separate elements into the general scheme of the creation, and

thus turn them into useful, cooperative forces supporting the
wishes of the Godhead. The task allotted to them was the creation
of the vessels of the divine *sefirot*, into which the divine lights
would later flow. The *shevirah*, therefore, was the rebellion of these
"different" elements that were left in the empty space, their refusal
to participate in the constructive process of creation, and their
successful achievement of a realm of their own in the lower part of
the *tehiru*. These elements, following the breaking of the vessels,
did not remain in their potential state; they now actively expressed
themselves, and are worthy of their proper name: the powers of
evil.

Following the *shevirah*, the cosmos was divided into two parts,
the kingdom of evil in the lower part and the realm of the divine
lights in the upper part. According to Luria, the essence of evil is
the opposition to existence; therefore it cannot exist by its own
power. In order to be, the evil powers must derive spiritual force
from the good divine lights. They achieve this by keeping captive
those sparks of the divine light that fell with them when the vessels
were broken, which thereafter give sustenance to the satanic realm.

Divine attempts to bring unity to all existence now had to
concentrate on the struggle to overcome the power of the evil
forces. This was done by a repeated process of divine emanation,
which first brought forth the system of the *sefirot*, and then the sky,
the earth, the Garden of Eden, and man were created. Man was
intended by God to serve as the battleground between the divine
forces of good and evil. In his essence Adam reflected symbolically
the dualism existing in the cosmos. He possessed a sacred, supreme
soul, while his body represented the forces of evil. The divine
intention was that Adam, by overcoming the evil in him and
making divine goodness victorious, would bring forth the downfall of Satan and all his realm. When Adam failed in his mission and
committed the first sin, a disaster followed, similar to the original
shevirah: instead of the divine sparks captive in the kingdom of evil
being saved and uplifted, many new divine lights fell down as a

result of Adam's action, evil became even stronger, and the victory of good over evil more remote and more difficult.

Instead of relying on the actions of one man, God then chose a people, the people of Israel, and allotted them the symbolic task of vanquishing evil and uplifting the captive sparks. The Torah was given on Mount Sinai to symbolize the Jews' acceptance of the task and their adherence to their part in the cosmic, mythological struggle. When the Jews said, "We shall do and we shall listen," expressing their complete subservience to divine goodness, the process was almost complete; redemption was imminent, and the forces of evil were almost defeated. Then the people of Israel created the Golden Calf, and this sin was the repetition of Adam's original sin. Again a fall occurred, the forces of evil were strengthened once again, and more and more sparks fell into the clutches of the servants of Satan.

History, according to Luria, is the story of the repeated attempts of the good divine powers to rescue the sparks and to bring unity to the earthly and divine worlds. Previous attempts had always failed. Luria and his disciples were absolutely certain that they were living in the last moments of the last attempt, which this time could not fail. They were sure that in their lifetime the process of the uplifting of the sparks was going to end, and that the coming of the messiah would signify the final success of the overcoming of evil, the mythological process that began with the *tzimtzum*. They believed that the people of Israel, and particularly the kabbalists of Safed, had an important role to play, and that they themselves, especially Luria and his disciple Rabbi Hayim Vital, had a messianic mission in this final stage of the cosmic drama.

While the myth of the contraction of God and the breaking of the vessels, the imprisoned and exiled divine sparks and the messianic expectations, created a revolution in the kabbalah, they do not seem to have had a direct bearing on the concept of ethics and its relationship to mysticism. The third element in Lurianic theology, the *tikkun*, is however, deeply connected with the emerging modern Jewish concept of mystical ethics.

VI

The concept of the *tikkun* is the most powerful idea ever presented in Jewish thought, which expressed an intense messianic endeavor of cosmic dimensions, and its consequences cover all aspects of the individual religious and ethical life. It was this idea that made Lurianic Kabbalah universally accepted by seventeenth-century Judaism in all countries, and had great impact on eighteenth- and nineteenth-century Jewish thought and practice as well. From the point of view of the subject of this book, the *tikkun* represents the complete fusion between Jewish mysticism and Jewish ethics, against the background of an intense Jewish nationalistic sentiment.

The term itself refers to nothing more than the "mending" of what was broken during the *shevirah*. After the catastrophe in the divine world, before the creation itself came into being, began the long and difficult process of the mending, which encompasses all history. Every historical disaster is a setback in the process of the *tikkun*, and every religious achievement assists in bringing it to a successful conclusion. As we saw above, the task of correcting the disaster in the celestial realm was put on the shoulders of the people of Israel. They are responsible for bringing about the terrestrial redemption and the celestial correction.

But how can man work toward the *tikkun*? How can man participate in the cosmic drama of the struggle between good and evil, and bring about the downfall of the satanic realm in which the earth exists? Luria's answer to these questions was based on early kabbalah and the ethical concepts of Moses Cordovero, but he went a few steps further than his predecessors.

The only weapon in the hand of man when he tries to assist the divine power in its mythological war against evil are the ethical and religious commandments, those listed in the halakhah, those described in ethical works like *Sefer Hasidim*, and the many new demands and customs introduced by the Safed community, including those initiated by Luria and his circle. All these deeds, as kabbalists have always maintained, are symbolic of divine processes, and in fulfilling them the individual participates in divine occurrences. Luria explained that each such deed contributes to the one and only all-consuming cosmic process of the *tikkun*.

The divine sparks that fell down and were captured by Satan in the many disasters throughout history can be redeemed by religious and ethical deed, claimed Luria. To each section of the prayers, to each benediction, to each charitable act, to each incident in the social life of every Jew, a spark is attached. If the Jew fulfills his duty and follows strictly the ethical and religious way, that spark is redeemed, freed from captivity, and uplifted to its source in the divine realm. When more and more sparks are thus freed, the kingdom of evil becomes weaker and weaker, for the divine sparks are the source of sustenance; without divine light evil cannot exist. When the process is complete and evil is empty of such captive sparks, it will simply crumble and vanish out of existence for lack of sustenance.

On the other hand, every time a Jew sins, thinks a bad thought, or commits an unethical act, a spark from his sacred soul is captured by evil, strengthens it, and joins those exiled divine elements which, uprooted from their place of origin, support the existence of evil. Each sin and each unethical deed has a divine spark attached to it in the individual's soul, and the sin plunges it into the abyss of the kingdom of Satan.

In this concept of the *tikkun*, Lurianic kabbalah gave a new meaning to ethics and to religious ritual. The seemingly endless demands of the halakhah and of ethical literature were not given by God merely to show the way toward individual salvation and an eternal life of bliss in the world to come for the individual. These precepts and commandments are the divine weapons in the cosmic struggle between good and evil, and no Jew can refrain, at any time, from taking part in it, whether he ever heard of Luria and his teachings or not. Every good deed always frees a spark, and every sin always strengthens evil. There is no neutral ground, there are no deeds or thoughts which do not contribute to one side or the other in this mythological strife. If a man is idle for an hour, he has missed an opportunity to uplift a spark. Idleness and idle thoughts certainly strengthen evil.

The intensity of Lurianic demands is most unusual. A person who accepts this world view and the ethical and religious consequences of the idea of the *tikkun* must always be under enormous pressure. Every mundane or apparently unimportant deed may carry endless cosmic meaning. A spark freed by charity now may be the last and only one, and the completion of the deed may bring forth the redemption immediately. Every evil thought or deed may spoil a cosmic achievement and plunge the world back into the state of *shevirah*, because if it were not committed, perhaps the world would have been redeemed. Accepting the Lurianic myth, one cannot help feeling that every deed (or misdeed) may decide the fate of the whole world, including that of the divine powers, for better or for worse. Ethical demands, therefore, assume an intensity of cosmic meaning and symbolical significance never before achieved in any Jewish ethical system.

There is another significant aspect to this concept of the correction of the disaster in the divine world. While following the ethical path in order to achieve personal religious perfection—as instructed by the Jewish philosophers, by the rabbinic writers, by the Ashkenazi Hasidim, or by the early kabbalists—is the lot of the individual, who does it alone and suffers alone the consequences of failure, Luria's system is a collective one. The correction of the *shevirah* is not in the interest of one individual more than another. If the aim is the freeing of all sparks—and only then will redemption come—then every deed of every Jew affects the lives of all other Jews.

Ethics in Lurianic Kabbalah is no longer an attempt to achieve personal perfection. It is a set of instructions directing the individual how to participate in the common struggle of the Jewish people. When he commits a sin, all suffer, because evil becomes stronger; when he does an ethical deed, everybody enjoys the resulting weakening of Satan and the enhancement of the redemption. Communal responsibility, an idea developed in Safed before Luria, is thus explained in religious and mythological terms. The individual's deeds are not his own private affair, because they profoundly influence the fate of the people as a whole. It is necessary, therefore, to supervise your neighbor's behavior, and if he strays from the right path to correct him and even to force him to follow the righteous way, because every one of his sins makes the task of the others more difficult.

It is impossible to combine this system with the modern concepts of the individual nature of religious faith and the freedom of the individual. Luria's *tikkun* created an ideology reminiscent of that of a fighting army: no one can say that he chooses today not to fight but to go to the theater because he is a free individual and has freedom of action. If he resigns from the struggle, the others have to do his part, and it is more difficult because they are weaker and the enemy becomes stronger. The duty of the correction of the divine upheaval rests on the shoulders of every Jew from the day he is born, and he cannot, in any way, evade it or shirk his responsibility.

In this way Luria brought a new meaning to the concept of repentance, again one that emerged in Safed before him. As long as religious and ethical perfection was the individual's aim, there was no place for repentance for anything but one's own sins. But when the responsibility is collective and communal, every Jew can and should repent because of the sins of everybody else, including past and future generations. There can be no end to the efforts one should make in order to free as many sparks as possible, because the task is universal and eternal and each individual contributes to it in the best way he can.

Lurianic Kabbalah can be perceived as the first modern Jewish nationalistic ideology. It allots to the Jewish people a unique task of cosmic dimensions, which can be performed only by them and which must be completed by them so that they will be redeemed. National salvation, not just individual perfection, is the end toward which ethical and religious efforts are directed. Every Jew will be rewarded, when the redemption is reached, by sharing in the collective, national salvation and not just by a personal reward from God. A fusion is thus achieved between the most far-reaching national goals and the most minute daily acts of ethical and religious righteousness.

In the first chapter we defined Jewish ethical literature as dealing more with the question "why" than with the question "what should be done." In this sense, too, the concept of the *tikkun* can be regarded as the maximum achievement of Jewish ethics. Anyone accepting the symbolism of Lurianic Kabbalah can have no more doubts concerning the reasons for the various ethical and religious demands of the Jewish way of life. Each act represents the redemption of a spark from exile in the realm of evil, and the totality of the process represents the redemption of the Jewish people as a whole from exilic existence, and the arrival of the messiah.

The Lurianic system also removed the sense of triviality and tediousness from religious and ethical behavior. Every repetition is not really one more prayer or righteous act; it represents the freeing of a new, fresh spark from its captivity. The intense struggle between the good God and Satan therefore gives fresh impetus to every old, mundane custom or demand. The forceful mythological symbols of the *shevirah* and *tikkun* make every deed meaningful for the individual, for the nation, and even for the divine powers themselves, for only human deeds can bring forth their purity and deliverance from the threat of evil.

The revolutionary nature of Lurianic mythology is obvious. The powerful new symbols represent a new departure in kabbalistic thinking. But at the same time Luria is the most orthodox thinker, whose ideas serve to fortify Jewish traditionalism. Though the symbols are new, the acts to be performed in order to achieve the tasks thus presented are the old, traditional precepts of religion and ethics, as presented by the halakhah and midrashic ethics. The novelty lies only in the sphere of the spiritual reasons for the performance of these demands; the demands themselves are not changed. Though Luria and his disciples did introduce several new customs to Jewish everyday practice of religion and ethics, the main body of deeds to be performed in order to achieve Lurianic aims is the traditional path of the Torah and *mitzvot*, of ethical behavior in one's society, family, and community, and the strict observance of all the commandments of Judaism.

Lurianic ethics spread very fast in the seventeenth century and became standard Jewish explanation of the ethical and religious demands of the halakhah. Almost all the works of ethics in Hebrew after 1620 use Lurianic symbolism, especially that of the *tikkun*. This concept spread into popular works, in which the details of Lurianic mysticism were not presented, but the basic notion that every ethical deed serves to mend what has been broken in the divine world and thus enhance the redemption was universally adopted. Lurianism became a national theology for Judaism for several generations.

Ethical literature, in this way, helped to integrate the revolutionary ideas and symbols of Lurianic mythological mysticism into Jewish tradition, and to infuse a new sense of urgency and meaning into the old ethical demands, while preserving the complete orthodoxy of the actions even though the reasons for them were new ones. Here we find one more example of the constructive role of Jewish ethics in absorbing new ideas and strengthening Jewish orthodoxy within the new framework.

CONCLUSION:
THE MODERN PERIOD

I

JEWISH ETHICAL LITERATURE has been presented in the previous chapters as the force that absorbed the revolutionary new ideas of philosophers, pietists, and mystics and turned them into a constructive and conservative ideology, which strengthened the spiritual power required to perform the demands of Jewish ethics and religious commandments. Can the same be said of the modern period? Was ethical literature a medieval phenomenon that performed its role in the Middle Ages but has had no relevance among the upheavals of modern times?

It is impossible in this brief chapter to give a detailed description of modern Jewish religious movements and their relationship to mysticism and ethics. But the thesis should be presented that, as far as traditional, orthodox Judaism is concerned, what was true in the Middle Ages is even more so in the period starting in the seventeenth century. The role of ethical literature, especially mystical ethics, only increased during these centuries.

The first example is that of the Sabbatian movement, the heretical messianism of the followers of Sabbatai Zevi, who converted to Islam in the year 1666. [1] After his conversion many of the followers of this messiah did not forsake him, but continued to believe in his mystical mission. Some of them were converted to Islam after him; others, in the eighteenth century, were converted to Christianity following Jacob Frank, a Sabbatian who claimed to be the incarnation of Sabbatai Zevi. But these were very small minorities. Most of the believers in Sabbatai Zevi remained Jewish and kept a secret their faith in a messiah who had already come—and converted to

104

Islam—thus, creating a "Sabbatian underground" within Jewish orthodoxy.

In the late seventeenth century and during the eighteenth century, many of the secret Sabbatian believers, who were gifted people actively participating in the spiritual and literary life of Judaism, accepted the paradoxical belief in the converted messiah. Many wrote books, some of which became popular and influential. On the other hand, some rabbis set out to discover the "hidden heretics" and expose them, and fierce controversies ensued.

The believers in Sabbatai Zevi were in fact Lurianic mystics who, following Sabbatai's prophet, Nathan of Gaza, introduced only one drastic change in Lurianism: though it is the duty of every Jew to participate constantly in the process of the *tikkun* by following Jewish ethics and ritualistic demands, and thus uplift the fallen sparks, they believed that the most difficult part of the task of the redemption cannot be accomplished by ordinary human beings. Only a divine power, incarnated in the figure of the messiah, can free the sparks locked in the innermost sphere of evil and thus redeem the Jewish people and the whole world. They believed that Sabbatai Zevi was that divine messenger, and that every Jew should support him by giving him his own faith as spiritual sustenance, so that he would be able to perform the great task that only he could do.

Sabbatianism, in this sense, is Lurianism in which the idea of the equality of every Jew in the face of the collective task of the *tikkun* was changed, and the idea of mystical leadership by an intermediary between God and man was introduced. The redemption cannot be achieved as a direct relationship between the Jews and God, but the mediation of the messiah, who receives the faith of the people and uses it to redeem the fallen sparks, is necessary. Thus the responsibility of the individual Jew in the face of the tremendous Lurianic demands is reduced, and the messiah is sent from heaven in order to achieve for him the most difficult part of the process of the *tikkun*.

Thus, Sabbatian writers, hiding their faith among orthodox

Jews, found no difficulty in writing works based on Lurianic theology, in which they had complete faith. Very often, however, they also included in their works some hints of their more radical Sabbatian beliefs. These hints were sometimes discovered by the opponents of Sabbatianism, and a controversy would break out, in which the author would vehemently deny his adherence to Sabbatianism. In other cases, the works were published anonymously in the first place.

This tendency toward secrecy can be illustrated by one of the most extreme examples: the fate of one of the greatest Jewish ethical masterpieces, the book *Hemdat Yamim* ("Joy of Days," meaning simply the Jewish holidays, the religious festivals). This book, which is homiletical in its presentation and includes homilies and instructions concerning all the festivals and days of fasting in the Jewish calendar, was printed in Turkey in the early eighteenth century. It was printed in four large volumes, one of the longest works in the history of Hebrew ethical literature. The printed edition did not include the name of the author, and it was regarded, and still is by most scholars, as an anonymous work.[2]

Some of the early readers of this work noticed that it included a liturgical poem which concealed in the first letters of its stanzas an acrostic—the name of the author—a common practice among Jewish poets. This signature read "Nathan," and was interpreted as referring to Nathan of Gaza, the prophet of the "messiah" Sabbatai Zevi and the leader of the heretical Sabbatian movement. Once this was recognized, other signs denoting the Sabbatian character of this vast work were easily found, among them the simple fact that though the book includes homilies and sermons for all Jewish festivals, there was one prominent omission: the Tisha' be'Av, the ninth day of the month of Av, the day of fasting in memory of the destruction of both the first and second temples in Jerusalem, which occurred according to Jewish tradition on that day. The ninth day of Av is not only a day of mourning and fasting in memory of this destruction, but is traditionally regarded as the birthday of the messiah, and indeed Sabbatai Zevi was born on that day. Among many sects of the believers in Sabbatai Zevi this day was regarded as a day of celebration and not of mourning, since the messiah has already come. Its omission from *Hemdat Yamim* is thus easily explained as a result of the author's wish not to include in his book sermons of mourning for this day, and he did not dare to reveal his adherence to Sabbatianism by expressing his true feelings concerning the day.

In many circles, therefore, *Hemdat Yamim* was regarded as a Sabbatian work. The Sabbatians were deeply hated by the Jewish establishment in the eighteenth century, for their heretical theology caused many hardships to the Jews, particularly after the Blood Libel, which was presented by the Sabbatian adherents of Jacob Frank in the disputation of Lvov in 1759, and the subsequent conversion of the Frankists to Christianity.[3] Still, *Hemdat Yamim* had great influence in almost all Jewish communities. There were some censures and attempts to abolish the book, but its influence remained, and remains to this very day, quite remarkable.

Modern scholars have investigated the problem of the authorship of *Hemdat Yamim*. A claim by Abraham Yaari that the book was written by a kabbalist in Safed who was not affected by the Sabbatian movement was criticized by Scholem and Tishby and proved to be incorrect. Recently Isaiah Tishby published a series of studies in which he discovered the sources of the book, hundreds of portions from other works, which were adapted in style so that they became an integral part of *Hemdat Yamim*, and the way in which it was composed. It seems that a group of rabbis in early eighteenth-century Turkey, led by the printer and publisher of the book, took part in its authorship in a most intricate manner. The book is actually the product of a conspiracy of a school of Sabbatian believers who jointly produced one of the best-written and most influential modern Jewish works of ethics.[4]

Its impact is felt in many fields. The great modern Hebrew writer, Shmuel Yosef Agnon, for instance, claimed that *Hemdat Yamim* was the main source of his unique Hebrew style. He was so influenced by this work that he not only named a central character in several of his stories "Hemdat," but also gave this name to his son. The Hasidic movement overtly forbade the use of the book, but many of its rabbis did use it in their homilies.

This is probably the clearest example of a Sabbatian work of ethics that was integrated within Hebrew traditional ethical literature even though its Sabbatian characteristics were known or at least suspected. The acceptance of *Hemdat Yamim* in no way represents acceptance or tolerance of Sabbatian heresy. But Jewish writers and preachers identified themselves so deeply with this genre of expression, ethics, and homiletics, that they could not bring themselves to reject it completely, even though they did not condone or forgive the heretical background of which they were aware. *Hemdat Yamim* remains to the twentieth century a part of Jewish traditional ethical literature, rather than part of Sabbatian literature.

Hemdat Yamim is not an exception, but represents several other similar phenomena. One of the greatest writers of ethics and homiletics in the early eighteenth century in Turkey was the author of *Shevet Musar* ("The Scepter of Morality"), Rabbi Eliyahu ha-Cohen ha-Itamari (i.e., from Smyrna). Each chapter of *Shevet Musar*, written in the form of a sermon, deals with an ethical value, and the book is one of the most important works of ethics to be written in that period. In addition to this popular work, which is one of the ten most influential Hebrew works of ethics ever written, Eliyahu ha-Cohen also wrote many other collections of sermons and ethical anthologies. It has been proved by Scholem that he was an adherent of Sabbatianism,[5] a fact that was undoubtedly known to many of his contemporaries. Yet his works lived and continue to live as an integral part of Jewish ethics, their importance undiminished because of the religious convictions of the author.

A similar story, connected with the biography of one of the most important and most fascinating Hebrew writers of the eighteenth century, is that of Rabbi Moses Hayyim Luzzatto of Padua. Luzzatto, an unusually gifted and prolific young man, gathered around him a group of adherents who believed in their messianic mission, adopting many Sabbatian ideas, even though they did not believe that Sabbatai Zevi was the ultimate messianic figure (this role was given to them by Luzzatto himself). They studied Kabbalah, interpreting it in a messianic manner, and wrote many messianic poems and kabbalistic expositions of their views. The news about this group reached the rabbis of Padua, and then of Venice, who demanded that they be disbanded and that Luzzatto undertake never to write any more kabbalistic works. Their demands were met, but a few years later Luzzatto was accused of breaking his promise, of adherence to Sabbatianism, and of witchcraft as well. He was forced to leave Italy, went to Amsterdam, and died a few years later at the age of forty, having immigrated to Eretz Israel.[6]

Besides his kabbalistic-messianic activity, Luzzatto, in his very short life, also wrote Hebrew plays, which, according to many scholars, begin the history of modern Hebrew literature. He wrote popular kabbalistic works, as well as books on language and rhetoric. He was not only a great scholar in Kabbalah and Jewish tradition, but one of the first Jews to be thoroughly familiar with the general non-Jewish culture around him.

While in exile in Amsterdam, Luzzatto wrote three works on Jewish ethics. All three were favorably accepted, but one of them, *Mesilat Yesharim* ("The Path of the Righteous"), became the most influential and popular Hebrew work of ethics. The book is organized into chapters that describe the ascent of the righteous, step by step, until they reach the maximum ethical and religious achievement possible for a man in his life. Luzzatto's style, the clarity of his exposition, and the profound religious spirit prevalent in the book made it preferred reading for Jews in almost every Jewish community in the world for nearly two centuries. In the religious academies of the Musar ("Ethics") movement in Lithuania and elsewhere in the nineteenth and twentieth centuries this book was learned by heart. Jews going on long trips by train used to take it with them as reading material for the journey.

The accusation of Sabbatian beliefs made against Luzzatto was no secret, and his banishment from his country as a result was a well-known fact. Yet the hundreds of thousands of readers of *Mesilat Yesharim* and his other works regarded it as irrelevant. The respect toward traditional Jewish ethics, and the deep-seated belief that there could be nothing wrong in such a work, was universal, and the acceptance of his teachings without checking whether there might be an element of heresy in them proves that to the Jewish mind, in the modern period as well as in the Middle Ages, heresy and ethical works cannot be combined. While Sabbatians were persecuted, and kabbalistic works were studied with great suspicion to determine whether they included any hint of Sabbatian heresy, the ethical works of well-known writers suspected of Sabbatianism were accepted as a legitimate part of Jewish tradition.

Another example is that of Rabbi Jonathan Eybeschuetz, the Rabbi of Prague, who was accused of Sabbatianism—and history proved the allegations true. A fierce controversy ensued, whose echoes were still heard even in the late 1900s. Yet the ethical homiletics of Eybeschuetz constitute a legitimate, respected part of modern Hebrew ethics.[7]

Sabbatianism, which expressed itself in mystical terms, brought with it controversy and strife in almost all aspects of Jewish life and thought. Yet the central place that Sabbatians held in the creation of modern Hebrew mystical ethics did not cause any stir in the quiet, orderly development of Jewish ethical thought and literature. The power of this literary genre to absorb new ideas and to cover eccentricities was as great in the modern period as in the Middle Ages.

II

Hebrew mystical ethics developed after the sixteenth century in four great steps: the first was the kabbalistic ethics of the Cordovero school; the second was Isaac Luria's revolutionary concept of the

tikkun; the third was the continuation of Lurianic mystical ethics in
spite of the Sabbatian upheaval, absorbing the ethical works of the
Sabbatians; the fourth was the appearance of the new Hasidic
movement in the second half of the eighteenth century.[8]

Hasidism is the only religious movement in Jewish history
which expressed itself almost exclusively by means of homiletical
and ethical literature. In the first thirty-five years in which Hasidic
works were printed (1780-1815), all the works written and printed
by the adherents of this new movement were compilations of
ethical sermons based on the terminology of kabbalistic symbolism, or ethical works written in the same way. The populariza-
tion of Jewish mysticism reached its final stage with this movement. It produced only popular works, and all its works were based
on the tradition of Jewish mysticism, though with many differences of emphasis and outlook. For Hasidim, religion and ethics
were one and the same, and ethical expression encompassed the
totality of their world view.

Hasidism is famous for its use of stories to express itself.[9] It
should be emphasized that this is a very late phenomenon, and its
dimensions are greatly exaggerated. Only in 1815, fifty-five years
after the death of the founder of the movement, Rabbi Israel Ba'al
Shem Tov, known by the acronym Besht, was the first book of
stories about him published, and the only other narrative work to
be produced in the first century of the history of Hasidism was the
collection of folktales by Rabbi Nahman of Bratslav. Only in the
last third of the nineteenth century did Hasidic tales begin to be
published in meaningful quantities, and even then most of the
writers and publishers were either non-Hasidim or former Hasidim
who did it for profit and not for faith. Ethical books, like the *Tania*
of Rabbi Shneur Zalman of Liadi, the founder of the Habad
(Lubavitch) movement, and collections of sermons and ethical
instructions, were the only literary genres used by the Hasidim to
express themselves and influence the masses.

The popularity of this literature undoubtedly enhanced the
spread of Hasidism and increased its impact, but it also served to

preserve the orthodox nature of the movement, which was suspected of heretical, and even Sabbatian, tendencies.

Even before Hasidic literature began to be published, a controversy broke out around this movement. Since 1772, for many decades, banishments of Hasidic communities, leaders, and books had been announced by the opponents of Hasidism, based on arguments that Hasidim neglected the study of the Torah and did not respect traditional scholars, but often masking a fear of a reemergence of Sabbatian heresy. The arguments sometimes became quarrels and caused so much hatred that Hasidic leaders were at times denounced, on religious and political grounds, to the Russian authorities, and in some cases were imprisoned. Until World War II the gulf between Hasidism and its opponents was so wide that in many communities marriage to a Hasidic family was forbidden. East European Jewry was caught in a religious schism, which only the Holocaust could overcome in the face of the common disaster.

In the late eighteenth century predictions of the opponents of Hasidism that this movement would prove to be a heretical one did not come true. Quite to the contrary, Hasidism today is probably the strongest conservative, traditional force in orthodox Judaism. Complete adherence to the minute details of the halakhah is a strict demand in all Hasidic sects. The study of the Torah, a life dedicated to talmudic scholarship, as well as insistence on traditional Jewish ethics are basic norms throughout the Hasidic courts in every country where Hasidism flourishes today, especially in Israel and the United States. Hasidism is a source of strict orthodoxy today, without the least hint of heresy.

Were the early opponents of Hasidism wrong? Were they mistaken when they discerned in the young Hasidic movement elements of future heterodoxy and heresy? This is one of the "if" questions that a historian is always careful to avoid. Yet the relevant facts should be presented, and the question of the role of Hasidic mystical ethics in the preservation of Hasidic orthodoxy should be assessed.

Hasidism appeared in the beginning of the second half of the eighteenth century in the same areas in which East European Sabbatianism had the deepest roots, and spread through the same masses among whom Jacob Frank, the great Sabbatian heretic who converted to Christianity, found his followers. The social stratum that produced many Hasidic teachers—the itinerant preachers and low-level intellectuals, who made a meager living from preaching in various communities, writing amulets, using folk medicine to heal the sick, driving away demons by prayer and magic, the *darshanim* and *ba'aley shem* ("masters of the holy name," by whose power they work magic)—was the source from which Sabbatianism acquired its aherents, and from which the early teachers of Hasidism emerged, including its founder, Rabbi Israel Besht.

These factors, though clearly external in character, were enough to arouse suspicion among the established rabbis and intellectuals of the great communities of East European Judaism. But in the teachings of the Hasidic movement there were even more elements which could be regarded as reflecting Sabbatian influence.

Two elements of Hasidic theology should be emphasized in this context. One is the common Hasidic belief, expressed both by the Besht and by his great disciple and the organizer of the movement, Rabbi Dov Baer of Mezeritch, that evil should not only be vanquished by its separation from the sparks of divine light that fell into it, evil should also be corrected and uplifted to its ancient roots. The source of evil is in the Godhead, and therefore it must originally have been good; if it is returned to its source, its character will change, and then not only will evil disappear, but the previously evil elements will now be contributing to the strengthening of divine goodness. Naturally, when the Lurianic command to vanquish evil by separation is strictly followed, orthodoxy ensues, because the righteous will try to remove every good element from the clutches of evil. But when the more ambitious task of correcting and uplifting evil prevails, there is the danger of coming into too close contact with its powers, a contact that may lead the righteous individual to fail in his task and become himself a captive of Satan, thus contributing to his power. (This is a similar problem to the one discussed above concerning Ashkenazi Hasidic ethics; whether it is better to take a risk by creating dangerous situations and overcoming them, or to stay away from circumstances that might lead to failure.)[10]

The opponents of Hasidism could discern in this ethical attitude not only ambition to achieve maximum mystical power by adding evil to the forces of goodness, but a hint of Sabbatian heresy, for the conversion of Sabbatai Zevi was interpreted by some of his followers as the result of the need to join the forces of evil in order to destroy them from within. Too close a connection between good and evil in the wake of the Sabbatian upheaval could be interpreted as preaching *"mitzvah ha-baah baevrah"*—redemption through sin in the Sabbatian manner. The fact known to us today, that these early Hasidic ideas did not develop to reveal their potential heretical power (and the further knowledge that similar ideas, or even more extreme ones, were written by non-Hasidim, as proved by M. Piekarz[11]) could not be known to the early opponents of Hasidism. Their apprehensions in the face of a new, popular movement with a suspect theology can be understood.

The second theological element in Hasidism that originated from Sabbatian theology is much more prominent and powerful: the idea of the *Zaddik*. This idea appears only in a general form in the works of the early Hasidim, but from the last decades of the eighteenth century it became the central theological as well as social phenomenon within Hasidism and distinguished this movement from all other segments of Judaism. Hasidim are organized, from the late eighteenth century to this very day, in the form of communities which adhere to a *Rebbe*, *Admor*, or *Zaddik*, who is the charismatic leader of the Hasidic group till his death, when his son or son-in-law usually inherits the responsibility and the title. The ideology behind this is that the common *hasid* cannot achieve the maximum possible religious status he deserves without some assistance from a divine source. This source flows to the community through the mediation of the *Zaddik*, who supplies his adherents with religious support and spiritual sustenance.

The *Zaddik* does not confine himself to spiritual matters; he assists the *hasid* in the choice of a wife and a profession, prays for him when he is sick, and promises him children if his wife is barren. In return, the *hasid* provides the *Zaddik* with two things: spiritual faith and material support. There is a delicate balance between the responsibilities of the *Zaddik* toward the community and those of the community toward the *Zaddik*.

It is not difficult to discover the origin of this idea. It is a transformation of the Sabbatian theology of the messiah into many small segments, confined in time and place. While Sabbatai Zevi was responsible for bringing redemption to the people of Israel and to the world, and the people owed him spiritual faith and material support while he strove to redeem them, the *Zaddik* is the "redeemer" of his community from everyday material and spiritual difficulties, assisted by the force of his adherents' faith. In both cases the basic idea is that of the existence of an intermediary power between man and God, an idea absent from Jewish thought till the appearance of the theology of Nathan of Gaza.

Hasidism certainly did not adopt Sabbatian theology. Rather it fragmented it, and the *Zaddik* is the "redeemer" and intermediary only with reference to the group that believes in him, and only during his lifetime. With some exceptions, he does not deal with cosmic messianic redemption, but with everyday problems of repentance and livelihood, sickness and sin. Yet the Sabbatian origin is present, and when a Hasidic group stops believing that anyone can replace its *Zaddik*, as happened when Rabbi Nahman of Bratslav died in 1810, or today in the Habad movement, then the redemption by the *Zaddik* develops cosmic proportions, and the identification of the *Zaddik* with the messiah is almost inevitable. The heretical element lies deep within the Hasidic concept of the *Zaddik* as a more-than-human intermediary between man and God.

Whether the early opponents of Hasidism were aware of the connection between the Hasidic theology of the *Zaddik* and Sabbatianism is uncertain; the persecutions of the Hasidim by its opponents started some time before the theory was developed and published and the social structure appeared. Yet they sensed that this new movement posed a threat to Jewish orthodoxy, and their suspicions did have some basis both in Hasidic theology and in the social organization of this movement.

The question is, why did Hasidism develop in such a strict, orthodox way? What caused it to hide and neutralize the potentially dangerous and innovative elements and concentrate all its considerable spiritual power in conservative teachings and way of life? It is the thesis of this essay that at least one of the reasons, and probably a major one, was the fact that Hasidism chose to express itself by ethical and homiletical literary genres, those old and well-tried methods that had throughout the Middle Ages and early modern times absorbed all novel ideas and turned them into orthodox, conservative ethical instruction.

The fact that all Hasidic teachings were presented not as theoretical speculations, in which an author develops his ideas according to their intrinsic power and follows the consequences of his basic presumptions, but rather as homilies, sermons, and ethical teachings, had a profound meaning. The great philosopher, Solomon Maimon, visited the "court" of Besht's disciple, Rabbi Dov Baer, in his youth, and in his autobiography described the manner of the Maggid's preaching. The lack of theoretical system, on the one hand, and the complete reliance on biblical verses, as well as the awareness of the specific circumstances of the moment, the characteristics of the audience, and their demands—all these, clearly portrayed by Maimon, explain why theoretical consistency was the last thing on the preacher's mind. All he wanted was to teach ethical maxims, using the centuries-old, traditional methods of ethical homiletics and instruction.

As in every "if" question in history, a clear statement fortified by philological proof is impossible in this context. But it seems that after following the development of Jewish mystical ethics through the ages, and observing the way that ethical literature successfully removed potential dangers of radical ideas and absorbed all the new kabbalistic and gnostic symbols and myths into constructive, traditional ethical norms, one has the right to suggest that the forces working within Hasidism were the same as those of previous Jewish mystical schools of thought.

The Hasidic movement, which since the early nineteenth century was pronounced by some critics to be in decline, is still forceful and thriving today. It reconstructed itself successfully after being driven away from Soviet Russia, and after the Holocaust, which decimated its adherents. Today most of the "courts," or communities, named after small towns in the Ukraine and Poland, are established in New York, Jerusalem, and Bney Brak, increasing its influence among orthodox Jews, and some Hasidic groups, like Habad, are trying to find ways to enroll non-orthodox Jews in its ranks.

The teachings presented by these Hasidic groups are those of Jewish mystical ethics, based on kabbalistic symbolism, including some elements of Lurianic *tikkun* myth and the theory of the *Zaddik*, which originated within Sabbatian mystical heresy. But the way these teachings are preached is the traditional way of Hebrew ethical and homiletical literature, combining interpretations of biblical verses with support from talmudic and midrashic sayings, and drawing from all aspects of Jewish culture, from *The Duties of the Heart*, originally a fiercely rationalistic work, to the *imitatio dei* notions of the school of Cordovero. All these are fused together into one traditional whole, its main message being strict adherence to the halakhah in every minute detail and dedicated observance of the ethical norms of Jewish social and religious ethics.

Hebrew ethical literature thus proved itself one of the principal vehicles of Jewish conservatism and traditionalism, continuing to develop in spite of all the drastic changes that modern history brought to the Jewish people: a complete change of geography, a new attitude toward non-Jewish culture, the advance of secularism, and, above all, the complete annihilation of the orthodox communities in Eastern Europe. Through all this, ethical and homiletical literature continues to educate new generations of orthodox Jews, who share the heritage of their forefathers in Gerona and in Mainz, in Safed and in Smyrna.

NOTES

Notes to Chapter 1

1. A general survey, including a detailed bibliography, of Hebrew ethical literature in the Middle Ages and early modern times is presented in my book *Ethical and Homiletical Literature* (Jerusalem: Keter, 1975; in Hebrew). Most of the material in this chapter has been discussed in that book, and therefore no detailed notes are added here.

2. The role of the believers in Sabbatai Zevi in early modern Hebrew ethical literature, seventeenth and eighteenth centuries, is discussed in chapter 5.

3. Another literary genre which approaches in its continuity and universality those of the halakhah and ethical literature is the Hebrew sacred poetry, the *piyyut*.

4. Concerning Hekhalot and Merkabah mysticism, see G. Scholem, *Major Trends in Jewish Mysticism* (2nd ed.; New York: Schocken, 1954), pp. 40-78, and his more specialized book on the subject, *Jewish Gnosticism, Merkabah Mysticism and Talmudic Tradition* (2nd ed.; New York: Jewish Theological Seminary, 1965).

Notes to Chapter 2

1. Jewish philosophy—its history, development, and major works in the Middle Ages—is described in two comprehensive studies: Isaak Husik's *Jewish Philosophy in the Middle Ages* (Philadelphia: Jewish Publication Society, 1948), and Julius Guttmann, *The Philosophies of Judaism* (New York: Holt, Rinehart and Winston, 1964).

2. Concerning the Ibn Tibbon family and its translations, see EJ s.v., and see below, note 40.

3. The wanderings of Rabbi Abraham Ibn Ezra and the locations in which he wrote his various works were studied by I. L. Fleischer in a series of articles in *Mizrah u-Ma'arav*, vols. 3-5 (1929-30). Concerning the contacts of Bar Hijja with the Jewish communities in Provence and elsewhere, see Friemann's introduction to his edition of *Hegyon ha-Nefesh* (Leipzig, 1860), p. 26, and the remarks by S. I. Rappaport on that subject in the same edition, pp. 38-40. Compare also G. Wigoder's introduction to the modern edition of this book (Jerusalem: The Bialik Institute, 1972), pp. 7-32.

4. On the history and development of rabbinic ethical literature, see Dan, *Ethical and Homiletical Literature*, pp. 146-66.

5. Concerning sixteenth-century Safed and the development of Kabbalah and kabbalistic ethical literature there, see note 4 to chapter 4.

6. On the ethical literature of the Ashkenazi Hasidim, see chapter 3.

7. It is clear that Rav Saadia, at least in this passage, regarded himself as opening a new field of teaching and speculation, without reliance on previous Jewish systemic treatment. On Saadia's ethics, compare I. Tishby's Anthology, pp. 7-40; Dan, *Ethical and Homiletical Literature*, pp. 16-21.

8. See Tishby's Anthology, pp. 77-108; Dan, *Ethical and Homiletical Literature*, pp. 21-25.

9. See the quotations in Tishby's Anthology, pp. 84-86.

10. On Gabirol's homiletics, see Dan, *Ethical and Homiletical Literature*, p. 25.

11. Detailed bibliography concerning this central work of Jewish ethics is included in Dan, *Ethical and Homiletical Literature*, pp. 273-75. For a brief discussion and summary of the problems concerning Bahya's biography, as well as bibliography, see Tishby's Anthology, pp. 109-110.

12. Sections of Bahya's introduction are included in Tishby's Anthology, pp. 123-25, and his discussion of the connection between prayer and study and the senses in Tishby's Anthology, p. 123.

13. Ibn Tibbon's translation of *Hovot ha-Levavot* into Hebrew was written in two parts; first, he translated only the first chapter dealing with God's unity, and only later the more specifically ethical nine subsequent chapters.

14. *Reshit Hochmah* by De Vidas is also one of the first works to combine kabbalistic ethics with Ashkenazi Hasidic ethics; see chapter 4.

15. S. Y. Agnon, *The Bridal Canopy*, chapter 1.

16. Gorfinkel's edition (New York, 1912); compare E. Schweid's detailed study on this work (Jerusalem: Iyunim, 1965).

17. See above, note 3. The scholarly works on *Hegyon ha-Nefesh* are listed in the bibliography to G. Wigoder's edition, p. 33.

18. See Dan, *Ethical and Homiletical Literature*, pp. 71-75, and Wigoder's introduction to his edition of *Hegyon ha-Nefesh*, pp. 13-18.

19. *Yesod Mora* was published by Z. Stern in Prague, 1833 (the first traditional edition was printed in Constantinople, 1530). On this work see I. Husik, *Jewish Philosophy in the Middle Ages*, pp. 187-96, and Tishby's Anthology, pp. 231-42.

20. Concerning Maimonides' *Sefer ha-Mada* and its relationship to Maimonides' philosophy, ethics, and law, see now I. Twersky, *Introduction to the Mishne Torah* (New Haven: Yale University Press, 1981).

21. On Nachmanides' life and work, see Scholem, *Ursprung und Anfänge der Kabbala* (Berlin: Walter de Gruyter, 1962), pp. 325-406, and E. Gottlieb, *Studies in Kabbalistic Literature* (Tel Aviv: Tel Aviv University, 1976), pp. 88-95, 569-70. The collected works of Nachmanides were published by H. D. Schevel in four volumes (Rav Kook Institute), which also include works attributed to him, like those of Rabbi Ezra ben Shlomo and Rabbi Jacob ben Sheshet. See Gottlieb's review of this edition in his *Studies in Kabbalistic Literature*, pp. 516-35.

22. Rabbi Jonah's life and works were studied by A. T. Schrock (London, 1948).

23. Rabbi Jacob ben Sheshet's two main works are his ethical treatise, *Ha-Emunah veha-Bitahon* ("Faith and Trust"), published in vol. 2 of Schevel's edition of the works of Nachmanides (because the book was sometimes attributed to Nachmanides, like several other works of the Gerona kabbalists) (Jerusalem, 1964). The second work, his anti-philosophical polemic *Meshiv Davarim Nekhochim*, was published by G. Vajda (Jerusalem: Israel Academy of Sciences, 1969).

24. On Rabbi Asher, see Scholem, *Ursprung und Anfänge der Kabbala*, pp. 348-50 and passim; E. Gottlieb, *Studies in Kabbalistic Literature* (Hebrew), pp. 62-70. His works were published by Rav Avida in *Ha-Segulah*, 1934-35, and again in J. Dan and R. Elior, *The Works of Rabbi Asher ben David* (Hebrew), with a detailed bibliography of the manuscripts of his treatises (Jerusalem: Academon, 1980).

25. On thirteenth-century Gerona, see I. Baer, *A History of the Jews in Christian Spain* (Philadelphia: Jewish Publication Society, 1961).

26. The kabbalistic center in Gerona was described by Scholem in *Ursprung und Anfänge der Kabbala*, pp. 224-349. Compare Scholem, *Kabbalah* (New York: Quadrangle, 1974), pp. 48-52 and his Hebrew book, *Ha-Kabbalah be-Gerona*, ed. J. Ben-Shlomo (Jerusalem: Academon, 1964). On Rabbi Ezra and Rabbi Azriel, see I. Tishby, *Studies in the Kabbalah* (Hebrew) (Jerusalem: Magnes Press, 1983).

27. On the Kabbalah in Provence, see Scholem, *Ursprung und Anfänge der Kabbala*, pp. 175-272, and Scholem, *Kabbalah*, pp. 22-28. His work in Hebrew on the subject is *Ha-Kabbalah bi-Provence*, ed. R. Shatz (Jerusalem: Academon, 1963). On Rabbi Isaac the Blind, see Scholem, *Ursprung und Anfänge der Kabbala*, pp. 219-30, and *Kabbalah*, pp. 42-47.

28. On Sefer Yezirah, see Scholem, *Major Trends*, pp. 75-77, and *Kabbalah*, pp. 21-29. See also I. Gruenwald, "A Preliminary Critical Edition of Sefer Yezira," *Israel Oriental Studies*, vol 1 (1977), pp. 137-77. Rabbi Isaac the Blind's commentary was printed by G. Scholem in his *Ha-Kabbalah bi-Provence* (Jerusalem, 1963), as an appendix. See on this text Scholem's *Ursprung und Anfänge der Kabbala*, pp. 240-55.

29. See below, note 40.

30. The book was published by G. Vajda, with notes by E. Gottlieb (Jerusalem: Israel Academy of Sciences, 1969).

31. On Rabbi Asher ben David, see below, notes 36-38.

32. G. Scholem, *A New Document Concerning the Early Kabbalah* (Hebrew) (Tel Aviv: Sefer Bialik, 1934), pp. 141-62. In this study (pp. 144-45) Scholem identified Rabbi Jonah Gerondi as the "Rabbi Jonah" mentioned in Rabbi Isaac the Blind's epistle.

33. See Scholem's analysis of this epistle in his *Ursprung und Anfänge der Kabbala*, pp. 219-29.

34. G. Scholem, *A New Document*, p. 143.

35. Scholem identified Rabbi Ezra and Rabbi Azriel as the targets of Rabbi Isaac's criticism; see *A New Document*, pp. 144-45. On the works of Rabbi Ezra and

Rabbi Azriel, see I. Tishby, *Mehkarim be-Sifrut ha-Kabbalah* (Jerusalem: Magnes Press, 1982); and G. Scholem, *Kabbalah*, pp. 48-50, 391-93.

36. Rabbi Asher's mission is described by Scholem in *A New Document*, pp. 143-45.

37. Rabbi Asher's text on the "Secret of Genesis" is found in Manuscript Paris no. 843, p. 92, and no. 823, pp. 179-81. It was published in Dan, *The Kabbalah of Rabbi Asher ben David* (Jerusalem: Academon, 1980), pp. 52-56. Rabbi Joseph ben Shmuel's text was published by G. Vajda in his edition of *Meshiv Devarim Nechochim* (Jerusalem: Israel Academy of Sciences, 1969), pp 193-95.

38. Rabbi Asher's text presenting this is to be found in his introduction to *Sefer ha-Yihhud* ("The Kabbalah of Rabbi Asher ben David," pp. 3-5).

39. This controversy has been the subject of many scholarly books and papers. A recent descriptive study with an up-to-date bibliography can be found in B. Septimus, *Hispano-Jewish Culture in Transition* (Cambridge: Harvard University Press, 1982).

40. *The Guide to the Perplexed* was translated into Hebrew by Rabbi Judah Alharizi and the definitive translation, which was accepted by all subsequent Jewish scholars and used as if it were the original work of Maimonides, was that by Rabbi Samuel Ibn Tibbon (the son of Rabbi Judah Ibn Tibbon, the translator of Saadia's, Bahya's and Ibn Gabirol's ethical works), Rabbi Samuel Ibn Tibbon was a philosopher himself, and wrote the rationalistic theory of the creation in his work *Ma'amar Yiqavu ha-Mayim*, to which Gerona kabbalist Rabbi Jacob ben Sheshet wrote his polemical answer, *Meshiv Devarim Nekhochim*.

41. Among the most important questions are those concerning the role of the rabbis in northern France and Germany in this controversy. See E. E. Urbach, "The Role of the Rabbis of France and Germany in the Controversy over Maimonides and His Works" (Hebrew), *Zion*, vol. 12 (1946), pp. 149-59.

42. Scholem discussed the role of the kabbalists in the Maimonidean controversy of 1232-35 in *Ursprung und Anfänge der Kabbala*, pp. 360-66. On Rabbi Jonah's role in the controversy, see Septimus, *Hispano-Jewish Culture in Transition*, pp. 63-70; Silver, *Maimonidean Criticism and the Maimonidean Controversy* (Leiden: Brill, 1965), pp. 150-53.

43. Concerning this legend see A. T. Schrock's monograph, *Rabbi Jonah ben Abraham of Gerona* (London, 1948).

44. See above, note 30.

45. The epistle was included in the collections of documents concerning the controversy. It was republished, with notes, in Schevel's edition of the works of Maimonides (Hebrew), vol. 1 (Jerusalem, 1963), pp. 336-48.

46. Nachmanides quoted a passage from Rabbi Eleazar of Worms's treatise on the unity of God to prove that the Jewish pietists in Germany, the most traditionalist Jewish movement in the Middle Ages, used similar terminology to that used by Maimonides in describing the unity of God and the absence of corporeal attributes in His being. See Schevel, vol. 1, p. 347, and compare Scholem, *Ursprung und Anfänge der Kabbala*, p. 360.

47. See the references above, notes 42 and 43.

48. This is evident especially in Nachmanides' homily on the Torah (Schevel, vol. 1, pp. 141-75, and especially p. 147).

49. Kabalat Rabbi Asher ben David (Jerusalem, 1980), pp. 3, 5, 10.

50. On this basic text of the Kabbalah, see Scholem, *Ursprung und Anfänge der Kabbala*, pp. 43-173. A German translation of the *Bahir* was published by Scholem in Leipzig, 1923, and reprinted in 1970 (Darmstadt: Wissenschaftliche Buchgesellschaft, 1970). A brief discussion of the book is in Scholem's *Kabbalah*, pp. 312-16.

51. Scholem, *Ursprung und Anfänge der Kabbala*, pp. 54-55, and *Kabbalah*, p. 315. Ibn Ezra's concept of the emanated divine glory probably influenced several sections of the *Bahir*, especially sections 128-34, according to R. Margaliot's edition (Jerusalem: Rav Kook Institute, 1951). A detailed discussion of this problem can be found in Dan, *Early Kabbalistic Circles* (Hebrew) (Jerusalem: Academon, 1977), pp. 92-97.

52. On the Provence kabbalists and their traditions, see Scholem, *Ursprung und Anfänge der Kabbala*, pp. 175-272, and *Kabbalah*, pp. 42-48; compare Dan, *Early Kabbalistic Circles*, pp. 144-59.

53. On the Rabad see I. Twersky's monograph, *The Rabad of Posquièrre* (Cambridge: Harvard University Press, 1962); on his mysticism see Scholem, *Ursprung und Anfänge der Kabbala*, pp. 180-200, and *Kabbalah*, pp. 43-47. See also Dan, "The Problem of Mystical Leadership," in *Leadership in Israel*, ed. E. Belfer (Ramat Gan: Dvir, 1981).

54. The appearance of popular mystical ethics in sixteenth-century Safed and its influence on seventeenth-century Jewish ethics in Eastern Europe is treated in chapter 4.

55. On this important author, see Dan, *Ethical and Homiletical Literature*, pp. 162-65, and 293.

Notes to Chapter 3

1. A detailed bibliography of texts and research concerning Ashkenazi Hasidism is included in Ivan G. Marcus, *Piety and Society* (Leiden: Brill, 1980), pp. 178-89. Marcus surveys the scholarly work done in this field on pp. 2-10.

2. A general description of Ashkenazi Hasidic ethics and mysticism was presented by Gershom Scholem in his *Major Trends in Jewish Mysticism* (New York: Schocken, 1954), pp. 80-118.

3. On this subject, compare Dan, *The Beginnings of Jewish Mysticism in Medieval Europe*, *History of the Jewish People*, *The Middle Ages*, vol. 2, *The Dark Ages* (ed. C. Roth) (Tel Aviv: Massada, 1966), pp. 282-90.

4. This tradition was published and studied in Dan, *The Esoteric Theology of Ashkenazi Hasidism* (Hebrew) (Jerusalem: The Bialik Institute, 1968), pp. 14-20.

5. Recently the historical problems raised by this document were restudied by

A. Grossman in his paper "The Migration of the Kalonymus Family from Italy to Germany," *Zion*, vol. 40 (1975), pp. 154-85. While Grossman is correct in raising some doubts concerning the accuracy of several details in Rabbi Eleazar's tradition, his conclusion that the whole story is a legend connected with the cycle of myths surrounding Charles the Great is much too radical. Charles the Great is not mentioned in Ashkenazi Hasidic literature, and they could not invent a family tradition just to praise him. There is no doubt that the genealogy and history of the Kalonymus family needs much more scholarly study.

6. Concerning Aaron of Baghdad, see *Megilat Ahimma'az*, B. Klar's edition (Jerusalem: Tarshish, 1944), pp. 13-26. His personality and traditions were the subject of a controversy between I. Weinstok, who attributed to him, in *Tarbiz*, vol. 32 (1963), pp. 153-59, several magical and kabbalistic texts, and Gershom Scholem, who proved (in the same volume, pp. 252-65) that there is no basis for such an attribution.

7. On this circle see my survey of their texts and theology in *Tarbiz*, vol. 35 (1966), pp. 349-72. On the legends concerning Joseph ben Uziel and Ben Sira, see Dan, *The Hebrew Story in the Middle Ages* (Hebrew) (Jerusalem: Keter, 1974), pp. 69-78, and detailed bibliography there.

8. See G. Scholem, *Ursprung und Anfänge der Kabbala* (Berlin: Walter de Gruyter, 1962), pp. 30-33.

9. The doctrines of this circle were described in detail in Dan, *The Esoteric Theology of Ashkenazi Hasidism*.

10. I. Baer, in his landmark study of this movement, "The Religious-Social Purpose of the Sefer Hasidim," *Zion*, vol. 3 (1938), pp. 1-50, suggested that the Ashkenazi Hasidic rabbis knew Latin and were familiar with contemporary Christian theology. Studies published in the last forty-five years have failed to find any proof of that. It is very doubtful whether they knew either the language or the theology written in it by the Christians around them.

11. Rav Saadia described the divine glory in the second chapter of his *Emunot ve-Deot* ("Beliefs and Ideas") (Leipzig, 1859), pp. 62-65.

12. Rabbi Judah the Pious's theological treatise, which objects to Saadia's views, was published in Dan, *Studies in Ashkenazi Hasidic Literature* (Ramat Gan: Massada, 1975), pp. 134-87; see especially p. 154.

13. Rabbi Judah the Pious's discussion of the revelation described in Exodus 33:19-23 is a commentary on Rabbi Abraham Ibn Ezra's description of this biblical portion in his *Yesod Mora* ("The Foundation of the Fear of God"), chapter 12.

14. See for instance Rabbi Eleazar of Worms's *Hochmat ha-Nefesh* ("The Wisdom of the Soul," i.e., Psychology) (Lvov, 1876), pp. 6d-7b.

15. The Ashkenazi Hasidic conceptions of the prayer are discussed in my paper, "The Emergence of the Mystical Prayer," in *Studies in Jewish Mysticism*, ed. J. Dan and F. Talmage, Association of Jewish Studies, Cambridge, Mass., 1981, pp. 85-120.

16. Concerning Nachmanides' epistle, see chapter 2, note 4.

17. The concept of divine immanence is discussed in detail in Dan, *The Esoteric Theology of Ashkenazi Hasidism*, pp. 84-104, 171-84. This concept was severely

criticized by a contemporary halakhist, Rabbi Moses ben Hisdai Taku, in his polemical treatise *Ktav Tamim*. See now my introduction to the facsimile edition of the Paris manuscript of this work, published by the Dinur Center for the Study of Jewish History, Jerusalem, 1984.

18. Rabbi Judah relied on the verse (Psalms 111:4), "a memory (i.e., hint) of His miracles." See Dan, *The Esoteric Theology of Ashkenazi Hasidism*, pp. 88-94.

19. Ashkenazi Hasidic demonology is the main source used by J. Trachtenberg in his *Jewish Magic and Superstition*, Jewish Publication Society, Philadelphia, 1939; compare Dan's *The Esoteric Theology of Ashkenazi Hasidism*, pp. 184-202, and its detailed bibliographical references.

20. This subject is described in Dan, *Studies in Ashkenazi Hasidic Literature*, pp. 34-43, and also Dan, "Samael, Lilith and the Concept of Evil in Early Kabbalah," *AJS Review*, vol. 5 (1980), pp. 27-32.

21. See G. Scholem, *Major Trends in Jewish Mysticism*, who pointed out the mystical elements in Ashkenazi Hasidic prayers and in their conception of the love of God.

22. Concerning Hekhalot and Merkabah mysticism, see G. Scholem, *Jewish Gnosticism, Merkabah Mysticism and Talmudic Tradition* (2nd ed.; New York: The Jewish Theological Seminary of America, 1965).

23. G. Scholem described this practice in detail in a special study, "The Idea of the Golem," included in his *On the Kabbalah and Its Symbolism* (New York: Schocken, 1965), pp. 158-204.

24. Dan, "The Emergence of the Mystical Prayer."

25. *Sefer Hasidim* (Frankfurt a/Main, 1924), par. 1673, p. 404.

26. *Hochmat ha-Nefesh* (Lvov, 1876), pp. 10c-d; and compare Dan, "Samael, Lilith and the Concept of Evil in Early Kabbalah," pp. 32-35.

27. Marcus dedicated three chapters to the subject in his *Piety and Society*, pp. 37-52, 75-86, 121-29.

28. Teshuvat ha-Gader is described by Rabbi Judah the Pious in *Sefer Hasidim*, section 37, p. 39.

29. The etymology of the term *teshuvat hava'ah* is unclear. The roots of the concept itself are to be found in the Talmud and were repeated by Rav Saadia Gaon.

30. *Hilchot Teshuvah*, the Roqeah (Jerusalem, 1960), p. 25.

31. *Sefer Hasidim*, sections 52-53, pp. 44-45; and compare my analysis in *The Hebrew Story in the Middle Ages* (Hebrew) (Jerusalem: Keter, 1974), pp. 176-79.

32. On the concept of the creator and his essences and immanence, see Dan, *The Esoteric Theology of Ashkenazi Hasidism*, pp. 84-104.

33. Many sections in *Sefer Hasidim* deal with this problem, but see especially section 14, pp. 13-15, probably a part of Rabbi Samuel the Pious's treatise.

34. This work was published by me in *Da'at*, vol. 2-3 (1979), pp. 99-120.

35. On the concept of the *zelem*, see Scholem's comprehensive study in his *Von der mystischen Gestalt der Gottheit* (Zurich, 1962), pp. 249-73; and on the Ashkenazi Hasidic views concerning it, see Dan, *The Esoteric Theology of Ashkenazi Hasidism*, pp. 224-29.

36. It should be emphasized that this solution to the problem is not presented clearly in the literature of the movement before us. My conclusions here are based on the various elements that comprise Ashkenazi Hasidic theology, when combined into a comprehensive system. It can be argued that the Hasidim did not devise such a system, and that contradictions exist unsolved within their various statements. Still, it seems to me that we have enough evidence to present the synthesis offered in the text above.

37. The clearest statement of this attitude is found in *Sefer Hasidim*, section 13, pp. 11-12. Similar ideas are found in Rabbi Eleazar's treatment of the subject of fear of God, in which he presents love of God not as an independent religious value but as the highest state of fear of God.

38. *Sefer Hasidim*, section 815, p. 206; and compare Rabbi Eleazar's description in *Sefer Raziel* (Amsterdam, 1701), p. 7b.

Notes to Chapter 4

1. Among the many studies on the circumstances and the results of the expulsion of the Jews from Spain, the most relevant one to the problem discussed here is H. H. Ben Sasson's study of how the expelled Jews viewed themselves, *Zion*, vol. 26 (1961), pp. 167-82; and compare his study in Baer Jubilee volume, *The Historical Society of Israel* (Jerusalem, 1961), pp. 216-27.

2. On the Marranos, see the detailed bibliography included in Y. Yerushalmi's *From Spanish Court to Italian Ghetto* (2nd ed.; Seattle: University of Washington Press, 1981).

3. Rabbi Joseph Ya'abez's views and those of other scholars of that period are described in Dan, *Ethical and Homiletical Literature*, pp. 180-89.

4. Safed, its atmosphere and its history, was described by S. Schechter in *Safed in the Sixteenth Century*, Studies in Judaism, 2nd series, 1908; see also R. J. Z. Werblowsky, *Rabbi Joseph Karo—Lawyer and Mystic* (2nd ed.; Philadelphia: Jewish Publication Society, 1975), especially pp. 38-83. A description of this community and a detailed bibliography are presented in Dan, *Ethical and Homiletical Literature*, pp. 202-35.

5. On the concept of the redemption in Safed, see below, pp. 80-82.

6. B. Talmud, *Sanhedrin*, p. 91b.

7. Maimonides, *Mishneh Torah*, Hilchot Melachim, 12:2.

8. See the comprehensive study by J. Katz on this controversy in *Zion*, vol. 16 (1961), pp. 28-45, and M. Benayahu, in "Sefer Zefat," *Sefunot*, vol. 6 (1964).

9. The most important stories about the exploits of Rabbi Abraham ha-Levi Beruchim are included in the fourth letter by Rabbi Shlomo Shlumil of Drezniz, published by S. Asaf in *Koves Al Yad*, vol. 13, pp. 118-31.

10. *Or Yaqar* is being published in Jerusalem by I. H. Elboim; twelve large folio volumes have already been published, and the work is far from being completed.

11. This work was translated into English and published with an introduction and notes by L. Jacobs, *The Palm Tree of Deborah* (New York: Hermon Press, 1974).

12. According to the talmudic exegesis of Exodus 34:6. See B. Talmud, *Rosh ha-Shanah* 15b.

13. This document was analyzed by G. Scholem in a special study described to it, published in *Zion*, vol 5 (1940), pp. 214-43.

14. Lurianic mysticism was described by Scholem in the eighth chapter of *Major Trends in Jewish Mysticism*, pp. 260-86, and in a special paper, "Kabbalah and Myth," originally published in German in *Eranos Jahrbuch*, vol. 17 (1949), pp. 287-334; an English translation is included in his *On the Kabbalah and Its Symbolism* (New York: Schocken, 1965), pp. 87-117. A detailed study of Lurianic mythology is presented in I. Tishby's *Torat ha-Ra veha-Kelipah be-Kabbalat ha-Ari* (Jerusalem, 1942; new ed. Jerusalem: Magnes Press, 1983).

15. Scholem, *Major Trends*, pp. 280-86, and I. Tishby analyzed especially the works of Rabbi Joseph Ibn Tabul; and when compared to those of Rabbi Hayim Vital, the essential Lurianic ideas can be reconstructed.

16. On the innovations of kabbalists in general and Luria and his disciples in particular in the field of Jewish customs, see G. Scholem, "Tradition und Neuschopfung im Ritus der Kabbalisten," *Eranos Jahrbuch*, vol. 19 (1950), pp. 121-80. An English translation is in *On the Kabbalah and Its Symbolism*, pp. 118-57.

Notes to Conclusion

1. The history of the Sabbatian movement is described in G. Scholem's monograph *Sabbatai Sevi: The Mystical Messiah*, trans. R. J. Z. Werblowsky (Princeton: Princeton University Press, 1973).

2. This work received much scholarly attention. A. Yaari dedicated a detailed monograph to an attempt to discover its author among the Safed kabbalists (Ta'alumat Sefer, Jerusalem: Rav Kook Institute, 1954), but his arguments were proven wrong by G. Scholem (*Behinot*, vol. 8, 1955, pp. 79-95). I. Tishby studied the book, its sources, and its historical background in a series of studies, the first two included in his *Netivey Emunah u-Minut* (Ramat Gan: Massada, 1964), pp. 108-68, and the concluding one published recently in *Tarbiz*, vol. 50 (1980-81), pp. 463-514.

3. On Jacob Frank and his movement, see G. Scholem, *Major Trends in Jewish Mysticism* (New York: Schocken, 1954), pp. 315-21; Scholem, *Kabbalah* (Jerusalem: Keter, 1974), pp. 287-309.

4. See note 2 above.

5. G. Scholem, *The Attitude of Rabbi Eliyahu ha-Cohem of Smyrna towards Sabbatianism* (Hebrew), Alexander Marx Jubilee Volume, The Jewish Theological Seminary of America, New York, 1950, pp. 451-70.

6. The messianic character of Luzzatto's group and their works were studied by

128   *Notes to Conclusion*

I. Tishby in a series of articles. A summary and bibliography are to be found in the *Encyclopedia Judaica*, vol. 11, pp. 599-604.

7. On Jonathan Eybeschuetz, see G. Scholem, *Kabbalah*, pp. 405-8.

8. See G. Scholem, *Major Trends in Jewish Mysticism*, pp. 325-50.

9. On Hasidic narrative literature, see my monograph, *The Hasidic Story* (Jerusalem: Keter, 1975).

10. On these ideas see I. Tishby and J. Dan, "Hasidic Theology and Literature," *The Hebrew Encyclopedia*, vol. 17, pp. 769-821.

11. Mendel Piekarz, *The Beginning of Hasidism* (Hebrew) (Jerusalem: The Bialik Institute, 1978).

INDEX